Dance
Teaching
Business

How Entertainment Transition Into Pedagogy & Entrepreneurship

Book #1

By José E. Espinoza

Disclaimer

Please note the information contained within this document is for educational and entertainment purposes only. All effort has been executed to present accurate, up to date, reliable, complete information. No warranties of any kind are declared or implied. Readers acknowledge that the author is not engaged in the rendering of legal, financial, medical or professional advice. The content within this book has been derived from various sources. Please consult a licensed professional before attempting any techniques outlined in this book.

By reading this document, the reader agrees that under no circumstances is the author responsible for any losses, direct or indirect, that are incurred as a result of the use of the information contained within this document, including, but not limited to, errors, omissions, or inaccuracies.

Dedication

To the Dance teachers, Entrepreneurs & Mentors of the New Generation

May your Legacy Live Forever

-   Jose E. Espinoza

Table of content

Jose E. Espinoza

Introduction

The rhythm of life beats with an irresistible allure, drawing us into the world of dance. It is a realm where passion meets precision, creativity intertwines with discipline, and art merges seamlessly with business opportunities. As you hold this book in your hands, you stand at the threshold of a universe that promises not just personal fulfillment but also professional success.

Picture this: a dimly lit stage, the quiet hum of anticipation in the air, followed by an eruption of movement as dancers take their first steps. Each twirl, leap, and pose tells a story that transcends words and captivates audiences. The beauty of dance lies not just in its visual splendor but in its power to connect deeply with people's emotions. For many, it's a lifelong dream to turn this passion into a career, to live each day immersed in the magic of movement. But how does one navigate the multifaceted dance industry to make that dream a reality?

This book is your guide, crafted specifically for young adults eager to combine their love for dance with entrepreneurial skills, for instructors keen to enhance their knowledge and business prowess, and for event promoters aspiring to host unparalleled dance events. Whether you're preparing for a future on stage or behind the scenes, there are abundant opportunities waiting for you.

The dance industry today is more dynamic than ever before, constantly evolving with new styles, techniques, and avenues of expression. From ballet to hip-hop, contemporary to ballroom, each genre offers unique pathways to success. Yet, beyond the glitz and glamor, the industry is also a robust ecosystem of dedicated professionals – choreographers, teachers, managers, marketers, and event organizers who work tirelessly to keep the heartbeat of dance alive. They all share a common goal: to create and sustain environments where dance can flourish.

Let's start by exploring the undeniable significance of the dance industry. Dance is more than just an art form; it's a cultural treasure and a universal language that bridges gaps between people from diverse backgrounds. It reflects society, champions causes, and leads movements. In many ways, it shapes and is shaped by the social fabric of our times. For those with the drive to excel, dance offers a platform not only to express individual artistry but also to influence the broader cultural narrative.

For young dancers, the promise of the industry is tantalizing. Imagine transforming your daily practice routines into captivating performances that leave audiences breathless. Picture yourself as part of a global community, traveling to far-off lands, attending prestigious events, and collaborating with the best in the field. The journey is demanding, filled with rigorous training and constant self-improvement, but it's also profoundly rewarding. With guidance on aligning your artistic talents with business acumen, you can carve out a niche that sets you apart.

Dance instructors, too, play a crucial role in this ecosystem. They are the mentors, the guiding lights who nurture raw talent into polished brilliance. Your ability to teach effectively can shape the next generation of dancers and inspire greatness. By expanding your understanding of the industry's business side – marketing your classes, managing finances, creating engaging curriculums – you can enhance your reputation and build a thriving dance school. Knowledge is power, and with the right tools, you can achieve lasting impact and financial stability.

Event promoters have a unique vantage point in this vibrant industry. If you're passionate about bringing people together and creating memorable experiences, promoting dance events could be your calling. Think about the excitement of organizing festivals, competitions, and showcases that highlight the best talent, foster community spirit, and offer entertainment to a wide audience. Success in this arena requires a blend of organizational skills, innovative thinking, and a deep appreciation for dance. This book will equip you with strategies to navigate logistical challenges, attract top performers, and ensure every event you host leaves a lasting impression.

While the road to success in the dance industry may seem daunting, remember that it's paved with countless stories of triumph. Every accomplished dancer once struggled with their first steps, every renowned instructor started small, and every successful promoter faced initial uncertainties. What makes a difference is the persistence to pursue your dreams and the willingness to learn and adapt.

Throughout these pages, you'll find insights, practical advice, and inspiring anecdotes designed to fuel your ambitions. You'll learn about the intricacies of building a dance career, from perfecting your craft and understanding market dynamics to developing brand identity and fostering meaningful connections. Each chapter is an opportunity to gain knowledge that will empower you to thrive in your chosen path.

So, as you embark on this enchanting journey, let optimism guide your steps. Embrace the idea that you can combine passion with professionalism, artistry with entrepreneurship, and creativity with commercial success. The dance industry is not just a space to work; it's a place to live your passion fully and unapologetically.

Welcome to a world where dreams take flight, where every pirouette, plié, and performance holds the potential to craft a remarkable career. The stage is set, the lights are on, and the music is cued. It's time to dance your way into the future.

PART 1:

Passion Into TALENT

Chapter 1:

Understanding the Dance Industry Landscape

Understanding the dance industry landscape is vital for anyone looking to thrive in this vibrant and ever-evolving field. This chapter delves into the foundational elements that shape the dance world, offering a comprehensive overview of its rich history, structure, key players, and the economic and social impacts it generates. By exploring these aspects, readers will gain a deeper appreciation of how dance has developed over time and where it stands today.

In this chapter, we first take you through the historical context of the dance industry, shedding light on how various dance forms have emerged and evolved across cultures. We then move on to examine the structure of the industry, highlighting the pivotal roles played by dance companies, academies, and influential figures like choreographers and dancers. Further, we'll discuss the economic contributions of the dance industry, including job creation and tourism, as well as its social impact, focusing on community engagement and cultural preservation. Finally, we address the challenges faced by the industry and explore future trends that could redefine its landscape.

Historical Context of the Dance Industry

As we delve into the historical development of the dance industry, it becomes evident that dance has always been an integral part of human culture and expression. From ancient rituals to modern performances, dance serves as a powerful medium to convey emotions, tell stories, and solidify community bonds. In various cultures around the world, dance is seen as both a sacred practice and a form of entertainment, highlighting its versatility and significance.

In ancient civilizations such as Egypt, Greece, and India, dance played a critical role in religious ceremonies and cultural traditions. Egyptian dance was deeply intertwined with their spirituality and mythology, often performed to honor gods and celebrate significant events. Similarly, in ancient Greece, dance was an essential part of festivities and theatrical performances, reflecting their reverence for the arts. Indian classical dance forms like Bharatanatyam have roots that trace back thousands of years, evolving through rigorous codification and maintaining their spiritual essence.

Moving through the ages, the evolution of dance styles and genres mirrors the dynamic shifts within societies. The Renaissance period marked a notable transformation with the emergence of ballet in the courts of Italy and France. Ballet became a formalized art form, characterized by its structured techniques and graceful movements. As it spread across Europe, it laid the foundation for various offshoots and influenced numerous other dance genres.

The 20th century witnessed a radical shift with the advent of modern dance, spearheaded by pioneers like Isadora Duncan and Martha Graham. Modern dance broke away from the rigid confines of classical ballet, embracing more expressive and natural movements. This era also saw the rise of jazz dance, heavily influenced by the rhythms and styles of African American music and dance traditions. Jazz dance brought a new level of excitement and spontaneity to the dance scene, setting the stage for future innovations.

Hip-hop emerged in the late 20th century as a cultural movement born from the streets of New York City. It encompassed not only dance but also music, art, and fashion. The dynamic and energetic style of hip-hop dance quickly gained popularity worldwide, influencing contemporary dance practices and even being incorporated into mainstream media and commercial performances.

Significant dancers and choreographers have left an indelible mark on the evolution of dance, shaping contemporary styles and practices. Figures such as Vaslav Nijinsky, who pushed the boundaries of ballet with his innovative choreography, and Pina Bausch, known for her avant-garde approach to dance-theater, revolutionized the field. Their contributions extended beyond mere performance, influencing generations of dancers and inspiring new forms of expression.

Embodying resilience and creativity, Alvin Ailey's establishment of the Alvin Ailey American Dance Theater in 1958 provided a platform for African American dancers and choreographers, showcasing their talent and celebrating their cultural heritage. His seminal work, "Revelations," stands as a testament to the power of dance in narrating personal and collective histories.

Understanding the major milestones and events that have shaped the course of the dance industry provides valuable context to its current landscape. The Paris Opera Ballet, founded in the 17th century, remains one of the oldest and most prestigious ballet companies in the world, playing a crucial role in the formalization and global dissemination of ballet techniques and repertoire.

The Ballets Russes, under the direction of Sergei Diaghilev in the early 20th century, brought together some of the most talented artists and musicians of the time, including Igor Stravinsky and Pablo Picasso. Their groundbreaking productions not only transformed ballet but also had a lasting impact on all performing arts.

The introduction of dance notation systems, like Labanotation developed by Rudolf Laban, allowed for the preservation and detailed documentation of dance works. This innovation enabled choreographers to share their creations globally and ensured that complex pieces could be accurately reproduced for future generations.

Television and film have also played pivotal roles in popularizing dance. Iconic movies like "West Side Story" and "Flashdance" brought diverse dance styles to mainstream audiences, inspiring countless individuals to explore dance themselves. Television programs such as "Dancing with the Stars" and "So You Think You Can Dance" have further democratized dance, making it accessible and entertaining for millions.

In recent decades, dance festivals and competitions have become vital platforms for showcasing talent and fostering professional development within the dance community. Events like the Helsinki International Ballet Competition and the Hip Hop International World Championships provide dancers with opportunities to gain recognition, network with peers, and secure career-defining opportunities.

Structure and Key Players in the Dance Industry

Dance is a vibrant and dynamic industry, encompassing various components and participants who play essential roles in its growth and sustainability. Understanding these key elements is crucial for anyone aspiring to build a career in dance. First and foremost, dance companies, academies, and institutions form the backbone of the dance industry. These organizations are pivotal in nurturing talent and promoting dance on multiple levels.

Dance companies serve as professional platforms where dancers can showcase their skills. They often perform across different venues, offering both classical and contemporary works. Companies such as Alvin Ailey American Dance Theater and the Royal Ballet have become household names, renowned for their excellence and innovative performances. Academies and schools, like the Julliard School and the Bolshoi Ballet Academy, provide rigorous training programs designed to refine technical abilities and artistic expression. These institutions also foster discipline, dedication, and a sense of community among dancers, preparing them for successful careers in the industry.

Prominent choreographers, dancers, and directors further propel the dance industry forward. Visionaries like Martha Graham, Pina Bausch, and Twyla Tharp have revolutionized dance with their unique styles and approaches. Choreographers create the movement vocabulary that dancers bring to life on stage, while directors oversee the creative direction and execution of productions. Their influence extends beyond individual performances, shaping trends and inspiring future generations of artists. Dancers themselves, such as Misty Copeland and Rudolf Nureyev, not only captivate audiences but also serve as role models and ambassadors for the art form.

Another critical aspect of the dance industry is the impact of dance competitions, festivals, and showcases on professional development. Events like the Youth America Grand Prix, the International Dance Festival, and local dance recitals provide platforms for dancers to gain exposure and experience. These events are opportunities for dancers to receive feedback, network with industry professionals, and potentially secure scholarships or contracts. Competitions and festivals also foster a spirit of camaraderie and healthy competition, encouraging dancers to push their boundaries and strive for excellence.

The collaborative nature of the dance industry cannot be overstated. Successful dance productions are often the result of partnerships between numerous professionals. Choreographers work closely with musicians to ensure the music complements the movement. Costume designers create outfits that enhance the visual appeal and functionality of the performance. Stage managers coordinate the logistics, from lighting to set design, ensuring a seamless production. This collaboration extends to other fields, such as multimedia artists who incorporate digital elements into performances, making the final product a rich, multi-sensory experience.

Economic and Social Impact of the Dance Industry

The dance industry is a vibrant and dynamic sector, contributing significantly to the economy and enriching society in various ways. One of the most evident economic impacts of the dance industry is job creation. From dancers and choreographers to costume designers, lighting technicians, and event planners, the industry provides employment opportunities across a wide range of professions. Dance companies, academies, and studios employ thousands of individuals, offering steady jobs and career paths for many. Beyond direct employment, the dance industry also supports ancillary businesses such as travel agencies, accommodation providers, and restaurants through events and performances that attract visitors, thereby promoting tourism.

Tourism driven by dance events generates substantial revenue for local economies. Major dance festivals and competitions draw participants and audiences from around the world, boosting hotel bookings, restaurant visits, and retail sales. Cities hosting these events often experience a surge in economic activity, leading to increased tax revenues and further investments in cultural infrastructure. The allure of unique dance styles and performances can be a strong selling point for tourist destinations, making dance an integral part of their marketing strategies.

In addition to its economic contributions, the dance industry plays a crucial role in fostering social cohesion and community engagement. Dance has the power to bring people together, creating a sense of belonging and shared purpose. Community dance programs and workshops provide accessible opportunities for individuals of all ages to participate in dance, promoting physical fitness, mental well-being, and social interaction. These programs often target marginalized or underserved communities, offering them a positive and inclusive space to express themselves and develop new skills.

Educational institutions also recognize the value of dance as a tool for holistic development. Schools and universities incorporate dance into their curricula to enhance students' artistic abilities, discipline, teamwork, and cultural awareness. Dance education encourages creativity and critical thinking, preparing young individuals to navigate diverse environments and collaborate effectively with others. Cultural preservation is another vital aspect of the dance industry's social impact. Traditional dances embody the history, values, and customs of different communities, serving as a living archive of cultural heritage. By preserving and promoting these dance forms, the industry helps maintain cultural diversity and fosters mutual understanding among various groups.

However, the dance industry faces several challenges that hinder its growth and accessibility. Funding is one of the primary obstacles. Many dance organizations rely on grants, donations, and sponsorships to sustain their operations, but securing consistent and adequate funding can be difficult. Economic downturns and shifts in public policy can lead to cuts in arts funding, forcing some organizations to scale back or shut down entirely. This lack of financial stability limits the industry's ability to support emerging talent and expand its reach.

Accessibility is another significant issue. While dance can have transformative effects, not everyone has the opportunity to experience it. Geographic, economic, and social barriers can prevent individuals from participating in dance programs or attending performances. Rural areas, for example, may lack the necessary infrastructure and resources to support dance activities, resulting in limited exposure and opportunities for residents. Similarly, high ticket prices and enrollment fees can make dance inaccessible to low-income individuals and families.

To address these challenges, the dance industry must explore innovative solutions and partnerships. Collaborations with educational institutions, community organizations, and private sector entities can help bridge funding gaps and increase access to dance. Leveraging technology, such as online classes and virtual performances, can also broaden the industry's reach, allowing more people to engage with dance regardless of their location or economic status.

Looking to the future, technological advancements and global trends are poised to shape the dance industry in exciting ways. Virtual reality (VR) and augmented reality (AR) technologies offer new possibilities for immersive dance experiences, enabling audiences to interact with performances in unprecedented ways. These technologies can also aid in dance education and training, providing realistic simulations and personalized feedback to enhance learning outcomes. Social media platforms have already revolutionized how dance is shared and consumed, allowing dancers and choreographers to reach global audiences and build their brands. Trends indicate that this digital transformation will continue to evolve, creating new opportunities for creative expression and audience engagement.

Moreover, the increasing emphasis on diversity and inclusion within the arts sector presents a promising outlook for the dance industry. As more organizations prioritize equitable representation and access, the industry is likely to become more inclusive and reflective of society's rich diversity. Initiatives aimed at supporting underrepresented groups, such as minority communities and people with disabilities, will help create a more vibrant and inclusive dance culture.

Sustainability is another area where the dance industry can make significant strides. As environmental consciousness grows, dance organizations can adopt eco-friendly practices in their operations and productions. This includes reducing waste, conserving energy, and using sustainable materials for costumes and sets. By embracing sustainability, the industry can contribute to broader efforts to combat climate change and promote environmental stewardship.

Core Message

As we've explored the foundational elements of the dance industry, it's become clear how deeply rooted and multifaceted this vibrant field is. From ancient cultural rituals to modern artistic expressions, dance has evolved through significant historical milestones, shaping both its artistic complexity and social relevance. By understanding the contributions of key figures and events, we gain a deeper appreciation of the art form and recognize the diverse influences that continue to inspire today's dance community. This rich history empowers aspiring dancers, instructors, and promoters to build upon a legacy of innovation and passion.

Looking ahead, the dance industry's dynamic structure offers numerous opportunities for growth and creativity. By harnessing the power of collaboration, technological advancements, and inclusivity, the dance world can continue to thrive and reach new audiences. Whether you're an emerging dancer, a seasoned instructor, or an event promoter, understanding these core aspects provides a solid foundation to navigate and contribute to the ever-evolving landscape of dance. The journey through the dance industry is filled with possibilities, and with knowledge and dedication, you can play a pivotal role in shaping its future.

Chapter 2:

Building Your Dance Skills

Building your dance skills is a multifaceted journey that requires dedication and an understanding of fundamental techniques. Aspiring dancers must focus on honing essential abilities such as balance, flexibility, and rhythm. These core elements form the foundation upon which complex dance movements can be built, enabling dancers to execute their routines with grace and precision. By developing these basic skills, dancers create a solid groundwork that will support them through more advanced stages of their training.

In this chapter, we delve into the specifics of each key component essential to proficient dancing. We start by exploring the importance of maintaining balance and how it influences a dancer's overall stability and control. From there, we address the role of flexibility in preventing injuries and allowing for a wide range of motion. Additionally, we discuss the significance of rhythm and its impact on synchronization with music. Finally, we'll look at the value of consistent practice, structured training schedules, and the benefits of seeking feedback from experienced dancers. The goal is to equip you with the knowledge and techniques necessary to excel in various dance styles and enhance your overall performance.

Developing Special Skills for Dance

Developing specific skills for dancing requires a well-rounded approach, starting with mastering fundamental techniques. Key elements such as balance, flexibility, and rhythm form the bedrock of proficient dancing.

Balance is crucial in dance. It allows dancers to execute complex movements with grace and stability. Improving balance requires strengthening core muscles through exercises like planks and leg lifts. Additionally, practicing poses that challenge your equilibrium, such as standing on one leg or holding a difficult position, can significantly enhance your steadiness. Ballet dancers, for instance, spend hours perfecting their relevé—a movement that requires them to rise onto the balls of their feet and hold the position. This not only trains their balance but also strengthens their ankles and calves.

Flexibility is another essential component. It enables dancers to perform a wide range of movements effortlessly and reduces the risk of injury. Daily stretching routines focusing on key muscle groups—hamstrings, quadriceps, hips, and back—can lead to significant improvements over time. Incorporating yoga into your training regimen can further enhance flexibility and overall body awareness. For example, hip-hop dancers often incorporate splits, high kicks, and fluid arm movements into their routines, all of which demand exceptional flexibility.

Rhythm is the heartbeat of dance. Understanding and internalizing the beat and tempo of music allows dancers to synchronize their movements seamlessly. Training your sense of rhythm can be achieved by practicing with metronomes, clapping to different beats, and dancing to various genres of music. Hip-hop dancers, for instance, rely heavily on rhythm to execute intricate footwork and syncopated moves that are hallmarks of the style.

Consistent practice and dedication are vital in honing these skills over time. Dancers who dedicate regular time to their craft see consistent progress. Establishing a structured practice schedule helps maintain momentum. Aim for daily sessions, even if they are short, to build muscle memory and refine techniques. During practice, focus on quality over quantity; executing movements correctly prevents the development of bad habits. Break down complex routines into smaller sections and master each part before putting them together. Remember, progress might be slow, but persistence pays off. Seeking feedback from experienced dancers can significantly accelerate skill development. Constructive criticism from those who have mastered the art provides valuable insights that self-practice cannot offer. Attend dance classes or join local dance groups where you can receive real-time feedback. Recording your practice sessions and reviewing them with a mentor or coach can reveal subtle mistakes you might overlook. Engaging in dance communities, both offline and online, can also provide support, inspiration, and opportunities to learn from others' experiences. For example, contemporary dancers often collaborate and critique each other's work to push creative boundaries and refine technical skills.

Diverse training can greatly enhance overall dance abilities. Cross-training involves incorporating different forms of exercise to improve strength, endurance, and flexibility. Activities like Pilates and swimming complement dance training by targeting different muscle groups and increasing cardiovascular fitness. Participating in workshops and intensives allows exposure to various dance styles and techniques. These sessions are usually led by experts who offer fresh perspectives and innovative choreography. For instance, attending a workshop focused on African dance can introduce new rhythms and movements that enrich your performance repertoire.

Workshops also foster creativity and adaptability. Learning a new style challenges the brain and body, keeping your training dynamic and engaging. By stepping out of your comfort zone, you develop versatility that sets you apart as a dancer. Furthermore, interacting with dancers from diverse backgrounds broadens your understanding of dance as an art form and inspires you to experiment with your own style.

Choosing a Suitable Dance Style

Selecting an appropriate dance style is a fundamental step for anyone looking to build a career in dance. Understanding the distinct characteristics of various dance styles can play a crucial role in determining which path to follow. Different dance styles offer unique attributes that appeal to diverse audiences and skill sets. Ballet, for example, is known for its grace, precision, and discipline. It emphasizes fluid movements, balance, and flexibility, and often tells a story through its choreography. Hip-hop, on the other hand, is dynamic and expressive, incorporating intricate footwork, isolations, and improvisation to convey energy and attitude. Contemporary dance blends techniques from modern, jazz, and classical ballet, allowing for creative expression and exploration of abstract concepts through movement.

Your personal interests and physical capabilities are significant factors when choosing a dance style. If you are captivated by a specific genre of music or culture, this passion can drive your dedication and enjoyment of the dance. Physical capabilities also play a role; for instance, those with natural flexibility might excel in ballet, while individuals with rhythm and quick reflexes may find hip-hop more suited to their strengths. Reflection on what brings you joy and aligns with your physical talents can help make the decision easier.

Specializing in a particular dance style offers numerous benefits. By focusing on one style, you can develop deep expertise and refine technical skills specific to that genre. This focused skill development can lead to mastery, making you a standout performer in that style. For example, committing to ballet can help you achieve exceptional balance and control, while specializing in contemporary dance can enhance your ability to convey emotion and create innovative choreography.

However, it's important not to limit yourself too early in your dance journey. Experimenting with multiple styles can be incredibly valuable. Trying out different genres helps you discover what truly resonates with you and broadens your versatility as a dancer. This experimentation also allows you to incorporate elements from various styles into your own unique performance technique. Dabbling in both hip-hop and contemporary dance, for instance, can make your choreography richer and more varied, combining the sharpness of hip-hop with the fluidity of contemporary.

To maximize your potential, start with classes in a few different styles. Observe how each one feels, how your body responds, and what excites you the most. Attend workshops, watch performances, and engage with communities within each dance genre. This exposure can provide insight and inspiration, helping you make an informed choice about where to focus your efforts.

Furthermore, consider seeking advice from experienced dancers and instructors. They can offer valuable perspectives based on their own journeys and observations of others' progress. Engaging in discussions with professionals can help you understand the demands and rewards of different dance styles, guiding you towards a well-suited choice for your goals and aspirations. Remember that selecting a dance style is not a one-time decision. As you grow and evolve as a dancer, your preferences and abilities may change. Stay open to revisiting your choice and exploring new directions as you gain more experience and understanding of yourself as a performer. Flexibility in your approach ensures that you remain passionate and engaged in your dance practice.

Lastly, embrace the journey of discovering your ideal dance style. Enjoy the process of learning and growth that comes with trying new things. Your enthusiasm and dedication will shine through in your performances, regardless of the style you ultimately choose. The key is to remain curious, committed, and true to what inspires you.

The Interdependence of Skill Development and Dance Style Selection

The journey of building your dance skills is not just about learning new moves but understanding how these skills interact with and influence different dance styles. Mastering fundamental skills such as balance, rhythm, and coordination can immensely ease the transition into a variety of dance forms. When you have a solid foundation, adapting to new styles becomes more intuitive. This groundwork allows dancers to focus on the nuances and unique characteristics of each style they explore.

For instance, a dancer proficient in ballet will find that their posture and balance skills translate well into contemporary dance. Ballet's emphasis on technique sharpens one's awareness of body alignment and control, which are essential across all dance forms. Similarly, hip-hop dancers who master isolations and rhythmic patterns can apply these skills when transitioning into jazz or modern dance. The versatility afforded by strong fundamental skills cannot be overstated; it gives dancers the confidence to experiment and grow.

Conversely, becoming highly proficient in a chosen dance style can further refine basic dance skills. Specializing in a particular style pushes dancers to perfect specific techniques associated with that form. For example, those immersed in tap dancing develop intricate footwork and an acute sense of timing and musicality. Over time, these specialized skills enhance overall dance competency, making the dancer better equipped to tackle other styles.

Dancers often merge different styles to create a unique performance identity, showcasing their broad skill set. One prominent example is Misty

Copeland, whose classical ballet training combined with elements of contemporary dance has created stunning performances. Another example is the duo Keone and Mari Madrid, known for blending hip-hop with theatrical storytelling, resulting in innovative routines that captivate audiences worldwide. Their success highlights how merging various styles can elevate performance quality and artistic expression.

Ongoing learning and adaptability are crucial components of both skill evolution and style exploration in dance. The dance world is ever-evolving, with new styles and techniques emerging regularly. Embracing continuous education through workshops, classes, and practice ensures that dancers stay current and versatile. Adaptability allows dancers to incorporate fresh elements into their repertoire, enhancing their overall performance and keeping their approach dynamic.

Moreover, adaptability fosters resilience. Dance is not just a physical activity but an art form that requires emotional and mental agility. Being open to learning and trying new things enables dancers to overcome challenges and setbacks, ultimately contributing to their growth and success.

To support this journey, it's valuable to seek mentorship and feedback from experienced dancers and instructors. They provide insights and constructive criticism that can help refine skills and broaden perspectives on different dance styles. Engaging in diverse training sessions, cross-training, and attending dance festivals can also significantly contribute to a dancer's development. These opportunities expose dancers to various techniques and styles, enriching their skill set and inspiring creativity.

Final Thoughts

Developing special skills in dance is a journey filled with dedication and consistent practice. We've explored how mastering balance, flexibility, and rhythm forms the foundation of proficient dancing. These fundamental skills are not only crucial for executing complex movements but also for preventing injuries and ensuring fluidity in performances. By setting structured practice schedules, seeking feedback, and engaging in diverse training methods like cross-training and workshops, dancers can continually refine their abilities and foster creativity, setting themselves up for success in various dance styles.

Choosing the right dance style is equally important as it aligns your passion and physical capabilities with your career aspirations. Experimenting with different genres helps you discover what truly resonates with you and broadens your versatility. Engaging with communities, seeking advice from experienced dancers, and attending workshops can provide valuable insights to guide your decision. Remember, as you evolve, so might your preferences. Stay open to exploring new styles and adapt to keep yourself inspired and engaged. This dynamic approach ensures that your dance journey remains fulfilling and allows you to shine in any style you choose.

Chapter 3:

Mastering Dance Performance

Mastering a dance performance requires more than just technical skill; it involves captivating the audience through presence, charisma, and emotional expression. Dancers must learn to project confidence and poise on stage, making their performance unforgettable. Building this stage presence starts with extensive practice and preparation, allowing dancers to become intimately familiar with their routines. However, confidence also stems from mental readiness, achieved through visualization techniques and maintaining a healthy lifestyle. These elements work together to prepare dancers both physically and mentally for their performances.

Throughout this chapter, we will explore various aspects that contribute to delivering a mesmerizing dance performance. You'll learn about the importance of facial expressions and body language in conveying emotions, making each movement resonate deeply with the audience. We will discuss the role of energy dynamics in keeping the audience engaged and how dancers can use eye contact and gestures to create an inclusive atmosphere. Additionally, we'll cover practical tips for event promoters and dance instructors, ensuring that everyone can benefit from these insights, whether they are performing, teaching, or organizing events.

Stage Presence and Charisma

Enhancing your presence on stage and engaging your audience effectively are pivotal aspects of delivering a captivating dance performance. It's not merely about the technical execution of the dance moves, but also about creating a memorable experience for the audience. Developing confidence and poise is foundational to achieving this level of performance.

Confidence isn't something that can be acquired overnight; it requires consistent practice and preparation. Regular rehearsals help dancers become more familiar with their routines, reducing the likelihood of mistakes during live performances. Practice sessions should involve mirror work, allowing dancers to observe and correct their posture, alignment, and movements. Additionally, recording rehearsals and reviewing them helps identify areas that need improvement and reinforces confidence in one's ability to perform flawlessly.

Preparation also includes mental readiness. Visualization techniques allow dancers to mentally rehearse their performances, picturing themselves executing every move perfectly. This mental practice can significantly reduce anxiety and boost self-assurance. Furthermore, maintaining a healthy lifestyle, including proper nutrition and adequate sleep, ensures that dancers are physically and mentally prepared for their performances, contributing to greater confidence on stage.

Once confidence is established, dancers must focus on using facial expressions and body language to convey emotions and connect with the audience. Dance is an art form that tells a story through movement, and facial expressions play a crucial role in communicating the narrative. A smile, a frown, or an intense gaze can express joy, sorrow, or passion, bringing the performance to life.

Body language complements facial expressions by adding depth to the emotional portrayal. Fluid arm movements, expressive hand gestures, and deliberate footwork can create a powerful visual impact. Dancers should practice these elements separately and then integrate them into their routines to ensure a seamless expression of emotions. Engaging in exercises like acting workshops can also enhance a dancer's ability to convey feelings authentically.

Understanding the importance of energy dynamics is key to ensuring continuous audience engagement. Energy dynamics refer to the variations in intensity and pacing within a performance. A dance routine that maintains a uniform level of energy from start to finish can become monotonous, causing the audience's attention to wane. Instead, dancers should incorporate dynamic shifts, alternating between high-energy, fast-paced sections and slower, more controlled movements. These fluctuations keep the audience intrigued and eager to see what comes next.

Additionally, dancers should be mindful of how they distribute their energy throughout the performance. Over-exerting oneself at the beginning can lead to fatigue, diminishing the quality of subsequent segments. Proper pacing allows for sustained energy, ensuring that the performance remains compelling from start to finish. Breathing techniques learned from practices such as yoga can help dancers manage their energy levels and maintain stamina.

Incorporating techniques for maintaining eye contact and acknowledging the audience is essential for creating a sense of inclusion. Making eye contact with audience members establishes a personal connection, making them feel valued and involved in the performance. It can be challenging to maintain eye contact while concentrating on intricate dance moves, so dancers should practice this skill during rehearsals. Identifying specific moments within the routine where eye contact can be naturally incorporated will make it easier to execute during the actual performance.

Acknowledging the audience goes beyond eye contact; it includes gestures like a nod, a wave, or an inviting smile. These small actions can make a significant difference in how the audience perceives the performance. They transform the dance from a one-sided display to an interactive experience. In group performances, synchronization in acknowledging the audience can amplify the effect, demonstrating unity and coordination among the dancers.

For event promoters and dance instructors, understanding these elements is equally important. Promoters can use this knowledge to evaluate potential performers and create environments that foster effective audience engagement. This might include designing stages that allow for better visibility and interaction or arranging seating to facilitate closer connections between performers and spectators. Dance instructors can integrate these principles into their teaching methods, emphasizing the development of both technical skills and expressive capabilities in their students.

Impactful Performance Techniques

One of the most crucial aspects of delivering a captivating dance performance is aligning your movements with the music. This concept, known as musicality, involves more than just dancing to the beat. It's about understanding the rhythms, melodies, and emotions conveyed through the music and reflecting them in your choreography. For instance, consider a piece of music that starts slowly but builds up to an intense crescendo. Your movements should mirror this progression, perhaps beginning with gentle, flowing motions and transitioning into more powerful, energetic steps. This alignment not only enhances the emotional impact of the performance but also creates a seamless connection between the dancer and the music. When executed well, musicality can turn a good performance into a memorable one, leaving the audience deeply moved by the synergy between movement and sound.

Next, we delve into the importance of spatial awareness. Utilizing the entire stage can significantly elevate a dance performance, turning it into a visual spectacle. Imagine a stage as a blank canvas waiting to be painted with your movements. Staying rooted in one spot may limit your ability to engage the audience fully. Instead, think of how you can move across different areas of the stage, create formations, and use levels—

both high and low—to add variety and maintain the audience's interest. For example, a solo dancer might begin at the front of the stage to establish intimacy with the audience and gradually move to the back to open up the space and invite a wider perspective. Groups can benefit from dynamic formations that change throughout the performance, ensuring that no two moments look the same. By being aware of your spatial positioning, you can create a performance that feels expansive and continually engaging.

In addition to movement and space, costume and lighting play pivotal roles in enhancing the visual appeal and thematic cohesion of a dance performance. The right costume can complement the style and story of the dance, adding another layer of meaning. For instance, flowing dresses might be perfect for a contemporary piece about freedom and fluidity, while sharp, tailored outfits could enhance a precise and powerful hip-hop routine. Lighting, too, can dramatically alter the mood and focus of a performance. Consider a dramatic spotlight highlighting a soloist during a poignant moment or colored lights that set the tone for different sections of the piece. Effective lighting design can guide the audience's emotions and draw attention to specific elements of the choreography. Together, costumes and lighting not only make the performance visually stunning but also reinforce its narrative and emotional content.

Storytelling through dance is perhaps one of the most profound ways to connect with an audience. Dance has the unique ability to convey complex narratives and evoke deep emotions without a single word. To tell a compelling story through dance, start by identifying the core message or theme you wish to communicate. Is it a tale of love and loss, a journey of self-discovery, or a commentary on social issues? Once the story is clear, use your choreography to illustrate this narrative. Every movement, gesture, and expression should contribute to the unfolding story. For example, a dancer portraying a character in turmoil might use sharp, erratic movements to symbolize inner conflict, whereas smooth, flowing motions could represent peace and resolution. Embedding a narrative within your performance adds depth and purpose, transforming it from mere entertainment into an impactful artistic statement.

Beyond these individual elements, the interplay between choreography, spatial awareness, costumes, and storytelling creates a cohesive and compelling performance. Each aspect supports and enhances the others, resulting in a well-rounded and unforgettable experience for the audience. For young dancers aspiring to build a career, mastering these techniques is essential. It demonstrates versatility and a deep understanding of what makes a performance truly special. Dance instructors can also benefit by incorporating these principles into their teaching, helping students appreciate the artistry behind every step. Event promoters, on the other hand, can recognize and select performances that exhibit these qualities, ensuring their events are of the highest caliber.

Final Thoughts

Developing captivating dance performances is about more than just mastering the steps; it's about creating a connection with the audience through your presence, confidence, and expressiveness. By focusing on mental and physical preparation, dancers can build the self-assurance needed to perform their best. Practicing facial expressions and body language helps convey the emotions of the dance, while understanding energy dynamics ensures that the performance remains engaging from start to finish. These elements, when combined, transform the technical execution into a memorable experience that resonates with viewers.

To take it further, using musicality and spatial awareness can elevate a dance performance to new heights. Aligning movements with music creates a seamless flow, enhancing the emotional impact. Utilizing the entire stage keeps the audience's attention and adds visual interest. Moreover, thoughtful use of costumes and lighting can magnify the narrative and emotional depth of the performance. Together, these techniques form a cohesive presentation that captivates and moves the audience. For young dancers, instructors, and event promoters, embracing these principles not only enhances individual performances but also elevates the quality of dance as an art form.

PART 2:

Professional

ACADEMIA

Chapter 4:

Becoming an Effective Dance Instructor

Strategies to Excel in Teaching Dance

Becoming an effective dance instructor involves more than just knowing how to dance well; it requires the ability to teach others in a way that fosters growth and learning. This chapter will guide you through designing a dance curriculum that not only facilitates learning but also ensures your students' continuous development. A well-structured curriculum is key to building a strong foundation for novice dancers, enabling them to master basic techniques before advancing to more complex moves. By starting with fundamental skills, you create a pathway for students to build confidence and proficiency one step at a time. This gradual approach not only makes the learning process more manageable but also keeps students motivated as they see their progress over time.

Throughout this chapter, you'll discover strategies for organizing your lessons to maximize student engagement and growth. We'll explore how to design progressive exercises that challenge students appropriately, introduce new techniques gradually, and incorporate regular assessments to track progress and adjust pacing. Additionally, you'll learn about the importance of setting clear learning objectives and tailoring content to different skill levels within your class. By the end of this chapter, you will have a comprehensive understanding of how to create a dance curriculum that not only teaches dance skills but also nurtures creativity, problem-solving, and personal growth in your students. This holistic approach ensures that every student, regardless of their initial skill level, can find joy and achievement in their dance journey.

Incorporating Progression

Designing a dance curriculum that facilitates learning in a step-by-step manner while challenging students appropriately requires strategic planning and thoughtful execution. The key to a successful curriculum is organizing lessons from basic to advanced skills to build a solid foundation. By starting with the basics, students can grasp the core techniques and movements essential for their dance style. This approach helps in creating a strong base upon which more complex skills can be developed.

For instance, in a ballet course, you would begin by teaching fundamental positions and movements like pliés and tendus. These foundational skills are vital as they recur in more advanced steps and routines. As students master these basics, their confidence grows, providing a sense of progress and achievement. It's important to regularly revisit these foundational skills, even as new, more complex techniques are introduced, ensuring that students retain their proficiency at all levels.

Introducing new techniques gradually is another crucial aspect. When learners encounter too much new information at once, it can lead to feeling overwhelmed, diminishing their confidence and enjoyment of dance. A gradual introduction allows students to absorb and practice each technique thoroughly before moving on to the next challenge. For example, after mastering basic ballet positions, you might introduce simple turns or jumps, giving students adequate time to practice and perfect these moves before combining them with others.

Incorporating regular assessments into your curriculum is essential for tracking progress and adjusting the pace accordingly. Assessments can take various forms, such as individual evaluations, group performances, or written tests on dance theory. Regular feedback from these assessments helps both instructors and students identify areas of strength and opportunities for improvement. This ongoing evaluation process ensures that students are neither bored by repeating material they've already mastered nor frustrated by being pushed too quickly through difficult concepts.

Progressive exercises are an effective method to help students apply learned skills in increasingly complex combinations. For example, in a hip-hop class, after students learn basic moves like the running man or the moonwalk, you can introduce sequences that combine these moves with new ones, creating dynamic routines. This progression not only reinforces previously learned skills but also encourages creativity and problem-solving as students figure out how to integrate different movements fluidly.

When designing your curriculum, it's beneficial to consider the overall journey of a dance student. Begin by outlining the end goals—what should a student ideally achieve by the end of your course? With this endpoint in mind, work backward to create smaller, achievable milestones. Each lesson should build upon the previous one, gradually increasing in complexity. This scaffolded approach ensures that students are continuously challenged without feeling overwhelmed.

Tailoring content to different skill levels within your class is also critical. Not all students will progress at the same rate, so it's important to offer variations or modifications of techniques that cater to varying abilities. For example, provide simplified versions of a move for beginners and more intricate variations for advanced students within the same class. This inclusivity keeps everyone engaged and fosters a supportive learning environment where students can learn from each other.

Communicating the purpose and relevance of each lesson helps keep students motivated. Explain how a particular skill fits into the larger picture of their dance education. For instance, showing how mastering turns can lay the groundwork for more dramatic leaps and spins in future lessons creates a sense of anticipation and purpose. Knowing the "why" behind what they're learning can drive students to put in the necessary effort to succeed.

Encourage students to set personal goals and reflect on their progress regularly. Personal goal-setting empowers students to take ownership of their learning journey. Simple things like keeping a dance journal or setting aside a few minutes after each class for reflection can help students internalize their achievements and focus on areas needing improvement. This self-assessment complements formal evaluations and promotes a growth mindset.

Additionally, fostering a positive classroom environment is essential. Create a space where students feel safe to take risks and make mistakes. Celebrate small victories and progress, no matter how minor they might seem. Positive reinforcement boosts morale and encourages students to keep pushing their boundaries.

Incorporating diverse teaching methods caters to different learning styles. Some students may thrive on visual demonstrations, while others benefit more from verbal instructions or hands-on correction. Balancing these approaches helps reach every student effectively. For instance, demonstrate a new move, describe it step-by-step, and then provide individual feedback as students practice. This multi-faceted approach ensures that all students have the opportunity to understand and master new skills.

Consider using technology as a supplementary tool in your curriculum. Online videos, apps, and virtual classes can provide additional resources for students to practice outside of regular class hours. Encouraging students to watch tutorial videos or participate in online discussions about dance techniques can reinforce learning and keep them engaged even when they're not in the studio.

Lastly, continuously seek feedback from your students. Their insights can provide valuable information on what's working well and what might need adjustment. Open communication helps build a strong rapport between instructor and student, making it easier to tailor your teaching methods to better suit their needs.

Setting Clear Learning Objectives

Setting clear learning objectives and outcomes for each lesson or course is an essential aspect of becoming an effective dance instructor. This practice not only ensures that your classes are well-structured but also keeps students motivated and on track towards their goals. In this section, we will explore the importance of defining specific goals for each class, establishing measurable outcomes to evaluate student progress, effectively communicating these objectives to students, and periodically revisiting and revising these goals based on feedback and data.

To begin with, defining specific goals for each class is crucial. Clear objectives give your lessons a sense of purpose and direction, helping you maintain focus throughout the session. For example, if you are teaching a beginner's ballet class, your goal might be to introduce students to basic positions and movements. By knowing exactly what you aim to achieve in each class, you can design activities and exercises that directly align with these objectives. This approach also helps in managing time effectively, ensuring that every minute of the class is productive and contributes towards achieving the set goals.

Furthermore, establishing measurable outcomes is vital for accurately evaluating student progress. Measurable outcomes serve as benchmarks against which you can assess how well students are absorbing the material and developing their skills. For instance, in a hip-hop dance class, a measurable outcome could be the ability to perform a specific routine by the end of the month. These outcomes can be assessed through various methods such as quizzes, practical exams, or performance reviews. Having concrete metrics allows both you and your students to understand where they stand and identify areas that may need more practice or attention.

Communicating objectives clearly to students is equally important. When students are aware of the expectations and the goals of each lesson, they are better equipped to align their efforts with those objectives. This transparency fosters a sense of ownership and commitment to their learning journey. Clear communication can be achieved through verbal explanations at the beginning of each class, written outlines, or visual aids like diagrams and videos. For example, before starting a contemporary dance class, you might explain that the day's objective is to master a particular technique or combination. Providing students with this context helps them stay focused and motivated throughout the class. Revisiting and revising objectives periodically based on student feedback and performance data is another key aspect of effective teaching. Dance is a dynamic field, and students' needs and abilities may evolve over time. Regularly soliciting feedback from your students can provide valuable insights into their experiences and challenges. This feedback, combined with performance data such as attendance records, test scores, and observations during class, can help you refine and adjust your objectives to better meet the needs of your students. For instance, if multiple students express difficulty with a particular move, you might decide to spend additional time on that aspect or modify your approach to make it more accessible.

In addition to these core practices, there are several strategies you can employ to further enhance the effectiveness of your teaching. One approach is to set both short-term and long-term goals for your students. Short-term goals, such as mastering a new step by the end of the week, provide immediate targets that keep students engaged and motivated. Long-term goals, like preparing for a recital or competition, offer a broader vision that encourages sustained effort and dedication.

Another useful strategy is to incorporate a variety of teaching methods to address different learning styles. Some students may respond better to visual demonstrations, while others might benefit more from verbal instructions or hands-on practice. By diversifying your instructional techniques, you can cater to the diverse needs of your students and enhance their overall learning experience.

Additionally, it's important to create a supportive and inclusive classroom environment. Encouraging open communication, providing constructive feedback, and celebrating achievements, no matter how small, can boost students' confidence and foster a positive learning atmosphere. Remember, the goal is not just to teach dance moves but to inspire and cultivate a lifelong passion for dance.

Finally, always strive to stay updated with the latest trends and developments in the dance world. Continuous professional development, such as attending workshops, taking advanced courses, and networking with other dance professionals, can enrich your teaching repertoire and keep your curriculum fresh and relevant.

In summary, setting clear learning objectives and outcomes is fundamental to effective dance instruction. By defining specific goals, establishing measurable outcomes, communicating objectives clearly, and revisiting and revising them based on feedback, you can create a structured and engaging learning environment that promotes student growth and success. Embracing additional strategies such as setting short-term and long-term goals, diversifying teaching methods, fostering a supportive classroom environment, and pursuing continuous professional development can further enhance your effectiveness as a dance instructor. Implementing these practices will not only improve your students' technical skills but also inspire and empower them to reach their full potential in the world of dance.

Whether you are a seasoned instructor looking to refine your techniques or a young adult aspiring to build a career in dance, understanding and applying these principles can significantly impact your teaching journey. Classes designed with clear objectives and measurable outcomes create an organized framework that makes learning dance a fulfilling and rewarding experience for both the instructor and the students.

Final Insights

Throughout this chapter, we have delved into the crucial elements of designing a dance curriculum that effectively promotes student learning and growth. By focusing on a step-by-step approach, starting with basic skills before gradually introducing more complex techniques, students can build a solid foundation while feeling confident and motivated. Regular assessments and feedback play an integral role in this process, providing valuable insights that allow instructors to tailor their teaching methods to meet the diverse needs of their students.

Moreover, fostering a positive and inclusive classroom environment is key to encouraging students to take risks and celebrate their progress. Incorporating various teaching methods to cater to different learning styles and leveraging technology for supplemental learning helps keep the classes engaging and effective. By setting clear objectives, continuously evaluating progress, and adapting based on feedback, dance instructors can create a structured yet dynamic learning experience. This approach not only enhances students' technical skills but also inspires them to pursue their passion for dance with confidence and dedication.

Chapter 5:

Marketing Yourself as a Dance Professional

Promoting your skills and services effectively is essential in the modern dance industry. For young dancers, instructors, and event promoters, knowing how to market themselves can make all the difference between standing out or blending into the crowd. In today's digital landscape, leveraging social media platforms like Instagram, Facebook, and TikTok allows for unparalleled outreach. By showcasing performances, tutorials, and engaging in live sessions, dancers can build a loyal audience and attract new opportunities.

This chapter delves into various strategies that dance professionals can use to enhance their visibility and connect with potential clients or collaborators. From posting diverse content, including solo and group dances, to collaborating with other industry professionals, we explore practical tips for growing your online presence. Additionally, the chapter covers the importance of offering workshops and private lessons as avenues to share your expertise and generate income. We also touch upon the value of networking and maintaining a consistent online presence to ensure sustained growth and engagement.

Creating a Personal Brand

In the competitive world of dance, establishing a strong personal brand is crucial for standing out and gaining recognition. Personal branding goes beyond just showcasing your talent; it involves creating a unique identity that differentiates you from others in the industry. This subpoint explores various aspects of personal branding and how they can enhance your marketability as a dance professional.

First and foremost, crafting your unique identity is essential. The dance industry is saturated with talented individuals, so having a distinct image can make all the difference. Start by identifying what makes you special. Are there specific dance styles or techniques that you excel at? Do you have a charismatic stage presence that captivates audiences? Reflect on these questions to discover your strengths and set yourself apart.

Once you've identified your unique qualities, developing a signature style becomes crucial. This style should reflect your personality and dance expertise. For instance, if you have a vibrant and energetic personality, incorporate those traits into your performances. Whether it's through your choreography, costume choices, or music selection, let your individuality shine through. Your signature style will become your trademark, making you easily recognizable to both fans and industry professionals.

Creating a compelling narrative is another powerful tool for personal branding. People are drawn to stories, and sharing your journey can help you connect with your audience on a deeper level. Think about your background, experiences, and challenges you've overcome. How did you discover your passion for dance? What obstacles did you face, and how did you triumph over them? Craft a narrative that resonates with your target audience. For example, if you're targeting young dancers, sharing stories of perseverance and dedication can inspire and motivate them.

To reinforce your brand, incorporating visual elements such as logos or color schemes is vital. Visual consistency helps create a memorable impression. Design a logo that represents your artistry and style. Choose a color palette that aligns with your personality and evokes the emotions you want to convey. Use these visual elements consistently across your social media profiles, website, business cards, and merchandise. This cohesion builds a strong and recognizable brand that leaves a lasting impact.

As you establish your personal brand, it's important to remember that authenticity is key. Be true to yourself and your values. Audiences can easily detect insincerity, so stay genuine in your interactions and content. Authenticity fosters trust and loyalty, which are essential for building a dedicated following.

In addition to authenticity, consistency is crucial in personal branding. Ensure that your messaging, style, and values remain consistent across all platforms. Whether it's your social media posts, videos, or live performances, maintain a coherent image. Consistency reinforces your brand identity and helps people recognize and remember you.

Networking also plays a significant role in enhancing your marketability. Attend dance events, workshops, and conferences to connect with other professionals in the industry. Collaborate with fellow dancers, choreographers, and instructors to expand your reach. Networking opens doors to new opportunities, whether it's performing in high-profile shows, teaching workshops, or even securing sponsorship deals. Building a network of supportive and influential individuals can significantly boost your career.

Furthermore, engaging with your audience is essential for personal branding. Respond to comments, messages, and emails promptly. Show appreciation for your supporters by acknowledging their contributions and feedback. Engaging with your audience builds a sense of community and fosters a loyal fan base. Utilize social media platforms to share behind-the-scenes glimpses, dance tutorials, and personal anecdotes. By involving your audience in your journey, you create a deeper connection and keep them invested in your success.

To ensure that your personal brand continuously evolves, seek feedback from trusted mentors, peers, and even your audience. Constructive criticism can provide valuable insights into areas where you can improve. Embrace a growth mindset and be open to learning and adapting. As you refine your brand, you'll stay relevant and continue to attract new opportunities.

Lastly, remember that personal branding is an ongoing process. It requires time, effort, and dedication. Keep refining your identity, honing your skills, and staying true to your values. As you grow and evolve as a dancer, so should your brand. Adapt to the changing trends in the dance industry while staying grounded in your unique essence.

Promoting Your Skills and Services Effectively

In today's digital age, promoting your skills and services effectively within the dance industry requires a strategic approach. One of the most powerful tools at your disposal is social media. By utilizing platforms like Instagram, Facebook, and

TikTok, you can showcase your talent to a vast audience through videos, tutorials, and live sessions.

Videos are an excellent way to highlight your dancing prowess. Posting clips of your performances or practice sessions allows potential clients and fans to see your skills in action. Make sure the content is varied – include solo performances, group dances, and collaborations with other dancers. Tutorials are another fantastic medium; they not only display your expertise but also provide value to your audience by teaching them new moves and techniques. Live sessions offer a real-time connection with your followers, allowing you to answer their questions, give advice, or even conduct mini-classes. Such interactions build trust and demonstrate your commitment to engaging with your community.

Engagement doesn't end with posting content. Interacting with your audience is crucial for building a loyal community. Responding to comments and messages shows that you value your followers' input and appreciate their support. When someone takes the time to leave a positive comment or ask a question, acknowledge it with a thoughtful reply. Engaging with your audience fosters a sense of belonging, making them more likely to share your content and recommend your services to others.

Another effective strategy is collaborating with other professionals in the dance industry. Cross-promotion opportunities arise when you partner with choreographers, dance instructors, or performers who have their own following. These partnerships can take many forms, such as joint performances, co-hosted workshops, or collaborative video projects. By working together, you can reach each other's audiences, expanding your visibility and credibility. Collaboration also introduces you to new styles and techniques, enriching your own skill set and broadening your appeal.

Offering workshops and private lessons is another avenue to promote your expertise while generating income. Workshops allow you to teach a larger group of people, providing a taste of what you offer. These events can be themed around specific dance styles, technique improvement, or choreography sessions. Private lessons, on the other hand, offer one-on-one attention, catering to individual needs and goals. Both options position you as an authority in the field and provide opportunities to connect personally with students.

When organizing workshops, consider topics that address common challenges or trends in the dance industry. For example, a workshop on mastering a popular dance style or improving stage presence can attract a wide range of participants. Promote your workshops through all available channels, including social media, email newsletters, and collaboration with local dance studios. Offer early bird discounts or limited-time offers to encourage sign-ups.

For private lessons, tailor your marketing to emphasize the personalized experience. Highlight success stories from previous students or share testimonials that speak to your ability to help dancers achieve their goals. Consider offering a free trial lesson or a discounted first session to attract new clients. Building a reputation for high-quality, personalized instruction will help you establish a steady stream of clients and referrals.

To ensure sustained engagement and growth, it's essential to maintain a consistent online presence. Regularly updating your social media profiles with fresh content keeps your audience interested and engaged. Experiment with different types of content, such as behind-the-scenes footage, interviews with fellow dancers, or insights into your creative process. Consistency helps you stay top-of-mind for your followers, making them more likely to think of you when they need dance-related services.

Building a robust email list is another powerful tool for promoting your skills and services. Offer a free resource, like a dance tutorial or a guide, in exchange for email addresses. Use this list to send out regular newsletters containing valuable content, updates on upcoming workshops, and special offers. Email marketing allows you to communicate directly with your audience, ensuring that your message reaches them without relying solely on social media algorithms.

As your online presence grows, consider investing in professional branding. This includes creating a polished website that showcases your portfolio, services, and contact information. A well-designed website acts as your digital business card, lending credibility and professionalism to your brand. Additionally, consider developing visual elements like a logo or color scheme that reflect your unique style and personality. Professional branding makes you instantly recognizable and reinforces your image as a serious dance professional.

Networking is another critical component of promoting your skills and services. Attend industry events, such as dance conventions, competitions, and workshops. These gatherings provide opportunities to meet potential clients, collaborators, and mentors. Be prepared with business cards and a concise elevator pitch that highlights your expertise and offerings. Networking helps you build valuable connections and stay informed about industry trends and opportunities.

Don't overlook the power of word-of-mouth marketing. Encourage satisfied clients and students to share their experiences with others. Positive reviews and referrals from trusted sources can significantly boost your reputation and bring in new business. Incentivize referrals by offering discounts or bonuses to clients who recommend your services to others. Word-of-mouth marketing is one of the most effective ways to build trust and credibility in the dance community.

Final Insights

Promoting your skills and services effectively requires a blend of strategy, creativity, and consistent effort. We've explored how utilizing social media platforms like Instagram, Facebook, and TikTok can showcase your talents to a broad audience through videos, tutorials, and live sessions. Building a loyal community involves engaging with your audience by responding to comments and messages, making them feel valued and connected. Collaborating with other professionals in the dance industry can expand your reach, while workshops and private lessons position you as an authority and provide opportunities for personal connections.

Maintaining a consistent online presence is key to staying relevant and top-of-mind for your followers. Regularly updating your profiles with varied content, from behind-the-scenes footage to interviews, keeps your audience engaged. Developing a robust email list allows you to communicate directly with your followers, offering exclusive content and updates. Investing in professional branding, such as a polished website and visual elements, reinforces your credibility. Finally, networking at industry events and leveraging word-of-mouth marketing can bring new opportunities and build lasting trust within the dance community.

Chapter 6:

Organizing Successful Dance Events

Organizing successful dance events requires more than just a passion for dance; it involves meticulous planning and attention to detail. From choosing the right venue that aligns with the event's theme to ensuring that all logistical aspects are covered, every element plays a pivotal role in creating an unforgettable experience for attendees. Whether you aspire to launch your own dance event or aim to enhance the success of existing ones, understanding how each piece fits into the larger picture is crucial.

In this chapter, we will explore the essential factors that contribute to the triumph of dance events. You'll learn about selecting venues that not only set the perfect atmosphere but also accommodate your audience's needs. We will delve into managing logistics efficiently, covering everything from acoustics and lighting to making the event accessible for everyone. Furthermore, the chapter will provide insights into contingency planning to ensure your event runs smoothly even when faced with unexpected challenges. By the end of this chapter, you will be equipped with practical tips and strategies to make your dance events not just memorable but also professionally executed.

Venue Selection

Understanding the critical aspects of choosing the right venue for successful dance events is fundamental to the overall success and appeal of your event. The venue you choose not only affects the atmosphere but also has a significant impact on logistics, attendee satisfaction, and ultimately the reputation of your event.

First and foremost, selecting a venue that aligns with your event's theme and caters to the audience demographics is crucial. For instance, a vintage-themed swing dance night would feel out of place in a modern, industrial-style hall. Instead, an old theater or a retro ballroom would enhance the historic ambiance and transport attendees back in time, making the experience immersive. Similarly, organizing a hip-hop event calls for an edgy, urban space where the aesthetics complement the vibe of the music and dance. Knowing your audience and understanding what appeals to them will aid in making informed decisions about venue selection. For young adults, trendy and contemporary spaces might be more appealing, whereas an older crowd might appreciate a more classical and elegant setting.

Ensuring that the venue size suits the expected number of attendees is another vital consideration. A venue too large for a small turnout can make the event feel empty and lacking in energy. On the other hand, a space that is too cramped can lead to discomfort and restrict movement, detracting from the enjoyment of the dancers. To avoid these pitfalls, it's essential to have a good estimate of the number of attendees when booking your venue. Consider whether there will be seated accommodations or standing rooms and ensure there is enough space for dancers to move freely. Overcrowded venues can also pose safety hazards, so adhering to occupancy limits and ensuring adequate ventilation is paramount.

The necessary facilities at the venue should not be overlooked as they play a significant role in enhancing the overall experience of your event. Restrooms, dressing rooms, and refreshment areas are some of the essential amenities that can significantly impact attendee satisfaction. For dance events specifically, having a proper dance floor is indispensable. A good dance floor should provide the right amount of friction to prevent slips while allowing smooth movements. Wooden floors are generally preferred by dancers over carpeted surfaces, which can cause tripping and hinder certain types of dances.

Moreover, consider whether the venue offers professional sound and lighting systems. High-quality acoustics are crucial for any dance event as they ensure the music is heard clearly and at the appropriate volume throughout the space. Poor sound quality can ruin the experience, no matter how talented the performers are. Equally important is the lighting setup, which should be able to create the desired mood and accentuate the performances. Flexible lighting options allow you to adjust the ambiance according to different segments of the event, such as dynamic lighting for upbeat dance numbers and softer, romantic lights for slower dances.

Tailoring the venue ambiance to match the event's mood is another imperative aspect that can elevate your dance event from ordinary to extraordinary. Ambiance encompasses elements such as décor, lighting, and even scent. For a salsa night, think vibrant colors, tropical plants, and string lights to evoke a lively Latin atmosphere. For a ballet recital, soft pastels, elegant drapery, and chandeliers may set a graceful tone. Sometimes, small touches like themed table settings, custom backdrops, and atmospheric lighting can transform a neutral space into a captivating environment, resonating deeply with attendees and leaving a lasting impression.

An important guideline to follow when selecting a venue is to conduct thorough inspections and walkthroughs before finalizing your choice. This hands-on approach allows you to experience the space firsthand, evaluate its suitability, and foresee any potential issues. During site visits, check every corner of the venue, test the sound system, and visualize how the event flow will work. It's also useful to take note of the location's accessibility to ensure all logistical needs, such as parking availability and public transportation links, are met for your guests' convenience.

Managing Logistics

Managing logistics for successful dance events is crucial to ensure that everything runs smoothly and attendees have a memorable experience. Proper planning and management of logistics can make or break an event. One of the primary considerations in this regard is the venue's factors, such as acoustics, lighting, and accessibility.

Acoustics are vital because they impact how music and announcements are heard throughout the space. Poor acoustics can result in distorted sound, making it hard for dancers to keep time with the music and detracting from the overall atmosphere. To address this, it's essential to assess the venue's acoustic properties before booking. Consider conducting a sound check or consulting with an audio professional to optimize the setup. This could involve adjusting speaker placement, using sound-absorbing materials, or investing in high-quality sound equipment to ensure clear and consistent audio throughout the event.

Lighting also plays a significant role in setting the mood and enhancing the performance. Good lighting can highlight the dancers' movements, create dynamic visuals, and elevate the entire experience for the audience. When planning the event, work with a lighting designer to develop a lighting plan that complements the performances. This includes choosing the right type of lights, their positioning, and coordinating light cues with the music. Whether you opt for dramatic spotlights, colored LED lights, or subtle ambient lighting, the goal is to enhance visibility and create an engaging visual experience.

Accessibility is another critical factor to consider. Ensuring that the venue is accessible to all attendees, including those with disabilities, demonstrates inclusivity and consideration for everyone's needs. This can involve providing ramps, elevators, and designated seating areas for individuals with mobility issues. Additionally, clear signage, accessible restrooms, and dedicated parking spaces for disabled attendees should be part of your logistical planning. By prioritizing accessibility, you make the event welcoming and enjoyable for everyone, thus widening your potential audience.

Coordinating transportation and parking arrangements for attendees is another logistical aspect that demands attention. Attendees need convenient ways to get to and from the venue. Providing clear information about public transportation options, offering shuttle services, or partnering with ride-sharing services can ease travel concerns for participants. For those driving to the event, ensure there are ample parking spaces available. It may be beneficial to negotiate reserved parking spots with nearby facilities or provide detailed maps and directions to parking areas. Efficient transportation and parking solutions reduce stress for attendees and contribute to a positive event experience.

Ensuring timely delivery and setup of equipment is essential for a seamless event. This includes sound systems, lighting rigs, stages, props, and any other necessary items. To manage this effectively, create a detailed timeline outlining when each piece of equipment needs to arrive and be set up. Communicate clearly with vendors and suppliers, confirming dates and times well in advance. It's wise to conduct a site visit with key team members to review the layout and logistics, ensuring everyone understands where and when equipment should be delivered and installed. Having backup equipment or spare parts on hand can prevent minor issues from escalating into major problems.

Planning for contingency measures is another critical component of managing logistics for dance events. Even with the most meticulous planning, unforeseen issues can arise. These might include technical malfunctions, weather disruptions for outdoor events, or last-minute cancellations by performers. Developing a comprehensive contingency plan involves identifying potential risks and devising strategies to mitigate them. For example, have extra generators or extension cords available if power issues occur. If an outdoor event faces inclement weather, arrange for tents or alternative indoor locations where possible. Develop a list of replacement performers or flexible program schedules to adapt quickly to changes. Training your staff and volunteers on these contingency measures ensures they are prepared to handle emergencies calmly and efficiently, contributing to a smoother event flow.

Real-life examples highlight the importance of these logistical factors. Imagine organizing a dance event where poor acoustics ruin the performances despite the dancers' best efforts. The audience leaves disappointed, and the event receives negative feedback. Conversely, picture an event with excellent sound quality, dynamic lighting, and seamless access for all guests. Transport options are clearly communicated, parking is effortless, and equipment is ready on time. The event runs smoothly even in the face of unexpected challenges, leaving everyone impressed and satisfied.

By considering the nuances of acoustics, lighting, and accessibility, along with efficient transportation and parking coordination, punctual equipment setup, and comprehensive contingency planning, you lay the groundwork for a successful dance event. These elements come together to create an environment where performers can shine, and attendees can fully immerse themselves in the experience.

Bringing It All Together

Planning and executing memorable dance events involves a detailed understanding of venue selection and meticulous logistical management. Throughout this chapter, we explored the importance of choosing a space that aligns with the event's theme and appeals to the target audience. We discussed how the right venue can enhance the overall ambiance and ensure a smooth event flow. From the vintage charm of a retro ballroom to the edgy feel of an urban space, selecting a suitable venue sets the stage for an immersive experience. Additionally, considering factors like accessibility, sound systems, lighting, and adequate facilities ensures that all attendees, including those with specific needs, have a positive experience.

Managing logistics effectively is just as crucial in creating successful dance events. We examined the impact of acoustics, lighting, and accessibility on both performers and attendees. Providing clear transportation options and ample parking can reduce stress and enhance the event's appeal. Timely setup and delivery of equipment are essential to avoid disruptions, while contingency planning prepares you for unexpected challenges. By paying attention to these details and maintaining a focus on the audience's experience, you can host dance events that leave lasting impressions, ensuring both enjoyment and success for everyone involved.

PART 3:

BUSINESS Beside Entertainment

Chapter 7:

Navigating the Business Side of Dance

Navigating the business side of dance is essential for anyone aspiring to combine their passion for dance with entrepreneurial skills. Establishing a successful dance studio or company requires more than just talent and enthusiasm; it demands a deep understanding of various financial aspects and strategic planning. From selecting the perfect location that attracts students to furnishing the studio with top-notch equipment, every decision impacts the overall success and reputation of your dance venture.

Considering factors like accessibility, foot traffic, and space requirements are crucial in making your studio a desirable destination for potential clients. Additionally, attention to details such as appropriate flooring, mirrors, and sound systems ensures a safe and professional environment where dancers can thrive.

In this chapter, we will delve into the essentials of setting up and running a dance studio or company from a business perspective. We will explore the importance of creating a detailed business plan that outlines revenue projections, expenses, and growth opportunities. Effective bookkeeping and accounting practices will be discussed to help you track income and expenses accurately. We will also examine different funding sources, including loans, grants, and investor partnerships, to provide financial support for realizing your vision. Finally, we will touch on pricing strategies that reflect the quality of your offerings while remaining competitive within the market. By understanding these key components, you'll be better equipped to navigate the business side of dance and build a thriving enterprise.

Setting Up a Dance Studio or Company

Finding the ideal location and space for your dance studio or company is the first and one of the most critical steps in establishing a successful business. The right location can significantly influence the accessibility and attractiveness of your studio to potential students and clients. Ideally, you want a place that's easily accessible by public transport and has ample parking spaces. High foot traffic areas like busy commercial districts or near schools and universities can provide an added advantage by drawing in passersby who may become future enrollees.

When touring potential locations, consider the layout and size of the space. A dance studio requires large, open areas with high ceilings to allow for full range of motion and movements. Mirror walls are essential so dancers can observe their form and technique. It's also crucial that the floors are appropriate for dancing—wooden sprung floors are often preferred because they offer the right amount of flexibility and reduce the risk of injuries.

Next, furnishing your studio with the necessary equipment and amenities sets the stage for a conducive learning environment. At the very least, a properly equipped dance studio should have ballet barres, sound systems, and adequate lighting. Depending on the types of classes offered, additional equipment such as mats, resistance bands, and portable mirrors could be required. Investing in quality equipment ensures not only the safety of the dancers but also enhances their overall experience, making them more likely to return and recommend your studio to others.

Beyond basic equipment, consider the amenities that will make your studio stand out. Clean, well-maintained bathrooms, changing rooms, and waiting areas are essential. Consider creating a welcoming reception area where parents or waiting students can sit comfortably. Adding small touches like free Wi-Fi, drinking water stations, and air conditioning can make a huge difference in how your studio is perceived. Your goal is to create a space that feels like a second home to your students—a place where they are excited to come back week after week.

Developing a brand identity and effective marketing strategies is another key component of attracting and retaining clients. Begin by identifying your unique selling points (USPs). What sets your studio apart from others? It could be a specific style of dance, the expertise of your instructors, or the quality of your facilities. Use these USPs to build a compelling brand story that resonates with your target audience.

Once you have a defined brand, it's time to get the word out. Leveraging social media platforms like Instagram, Facebook, and TikTok can be incredibly effective for promoting your studio. Share engaging content such as behind-the-scenes videos, testimonials from students, and highlights from classes or performances. Collaborating with local influencers or running promotions through these platforms can help you reach a broader audience. Additionally, having a user-friendly website with clear information about class schedules, pricing, and online registration options can make it easier for potential clients to take the next step.

Traditional marketing methods shouldn't be overlooked either. Flyer distributions in local schools, community centers, and nearby businesses can drive awareness. Hosting open house events where potential students can visit the studio, meet the instructors, and even try out a free class can convert curious individuals into committed members. Offering introductory discounts or referral bonuses can also incentivize sign-ups and help grow your student base organically.

Exploring legal requirements, permits, and insurance is vital for laying a secure foundation for your business. Start by researching the specific regulations in your city, state, or country. You'll need to obtain a business license and possibly some special permits depending on the nature of your studio's activities. These might include health and safety inspections, zoning permits, or noise regulations.

Insurance is another essential aspect that cannot be ignored. General liability insurance will protect you against claims resulting from accidents or injuries that occur on your premises. Professional liability insurance is advisable for covering claims related to the instruction itself, such as cases where a student might blame an injury on negligence or improper teaching techniques. Worker's compensation insurance is also necessary if you have employees, which is likely given that most dance studios employ multiple instructors and administrative staff.

Legal considerations extend beyond permits and insurance. Drafting clear contracts for students and staff can prevent misunderstandings and protect your interests. Student contracts should outline class policies, payment terms, and cancellation procedures. Instructor contracts should detail job responsibilities, salary or pay structure, and non-compete clauses to ensure that your investment in staff training won't lead to them opening competing studios across the street.

Moreover, never underestimate the importance of intellectual property law. Your studio's name, logo, and any unique program names you've developed should be trademarked to prevent unauthorized use by competitors. If you're producing original choreographies and performance pieces, consider copyrighting these works to safeguard your creative assets.

Financial Planning and Management

When venturing into the business side of dance, financial planning and management are crucial components for success. Creating a detailed business plan is the first step towards building a sustainable dance studio or company. This plan should encompass revenue projections, expenses, and growth opportunities. Begin by identifying your potential sources of income. These could include tuition fees from classes, ticket sales from performances, merchandise, and even rental income if you have space to sublet. Accurately estimating these revenues will provide a clear picture of the financial health of your business.

Next, outline all projected expenses. This includes both fixed and variable costs such as rent, utilities, salaries, marketing, costumes, and equipment. It's essential to account for every possible expense, no matter how small, to avoid unexpected financial strain. Additionally, consider potential growth opportunities. Are there ways to expand your offerings, such as adding new classes, hosting workshops, or engaging in community events? Including these possibilities in your business plan can help you set realistic goals and strategies for scaling your operations over time.

Once your business plan is established, implementing effective bookkeeping and accounting practices is vital for tracking income, expenses, and profitability. Regularly updating your books ensures that you maintain a clear and accurate financial record, which is imperative for making informed decisions. Utilize accounting software designed for small businesses to streamline this process. Recording each transaction meticulously helps in understanding cash flow patterns, identifying financial trends, and preparing for tax season. Hiring a professional accountant or bookkeeper can also be beneficial, especially if you're less familiar with financial management.

Another crucial aspect of financial planning is identifying funding sources. While personal savings may be a starting point, additional funds might be necessary to fully realize your vision. Exploring various funding options like loans, grants, and investor partnerships can provide the financial support needed to grow your business. Government and private grants specifically aimed at the arts can be a valuable resource. Similarly, forming partnerships with investors who share your passion for dance can bring not only financial backing but also strategic advice and networking opportunities. Each funding source comes with its own set of requirements and implications, so it's important to thoroughly research and evaluate which options align best with your business goals.

Establishing pricing strategies for your services is another key element in ensuring the financial sustainability of your dance studio or company. Pricing should reflect the quality and uniqueness of what you offer, while also being competitive within the market. Start by researching the pricing structures of similar studios in your area. Consider the demographics of your target audience and their willingness to pay. For instance, offering tiered pricing for different levels of class difficulty, membership packages, or discounts for early registration can attract a wider range of students. Additionally, think about hosting special events or masterclasses with higher pricing to boost your revenue streams periodically.

To maximize profitability, it's beneficial to continually reassess and adjust your pricing strategy based on feedback and market changes. Gathering input from your students and attendees through surveys can provide insight into their perception of value for money. Adjusting prices accordingly can help retain current clients and attract new ones. Moreover, transparent communication about any price changes, along with the added value they bring, fosters trust and loyalty among your clientele.

Operational Efficiency and Sustainability

Enhancing operational efficiency and ensuring long-term sustainability for a dance studio or company are essential for thriving in the competitive dance industry. A significant way to achieve this is by streamlining administrative processes through the use of management software and systems. These tools can help automate tasks such as scheduling, billing, and communication with students and parents. By reducing the time spent on routine administrative tasks, studio owners and managers can focus more on strategic planning and improving the quality of their offerings.

For instance, using an integrated management system can simplify class enrolments, track attendance, and even manage staff payroll. This not only enhances efficiency but also reduces the likelihood of human error. Moreover, adopting digital solutions can provide valuable insights through data analytics, helping you to understand trends in student attendance and preferences. This information can guide decision-making, from adjusting class schedules to devising promotional strategies, ultimately leading to a more responsive and adaptive business model.

Developing a team of qualified instructors and staff is another cornerstone of maintaining high standards of teaching and customer service. Hiring experienced professionals who are not only skilled dancers but also effective teachers is crucial. It's beneficial to invest in ongoing training and professional development for your staff. Workshops, certifications, and industry conferences can keep them updated on the latest teaching techniques and trends in dance education.

Creating a supportive and collaborative work environment is also important. Encouraging open communication and providing opportunities for staff to share their ideas can foster a sense of ownership and commitment. Additionally, recognizing and rewarding outstanding performance can boost morale and motivate your team to maintain high standards. High-quality instruction leads to satisfied students, which in turn builds a strong reputation for your studio, attracting new clients and retaining existing ones.

Community engagement initiatives and partnerships play a vital role in building a loyal client base. Participating in local events, offering free workshops, or hosting open house days can increase visibility and attract potential students. Partnering with schools, community centers, and local businesses can create mutually beneficial relationships. For example, collaborating with a local fitness center can lead to cross-promotional opportunities where their members receive discounts on dance classes and vice versa.

Another effective strategy is to leverage social media and online marketing. Creating engaging content that showcases your studio's activities, success stories, and upcoming events can help build an online community. Regularly interacting with followers by responding to comments and messages creates a more personal connection, making people feel valued and part of the dance family. Online reviews and testimonials can also serve as powerful tools for attracting new students.

Adopting green practices and sustainability measures reduces the environmental impact of your business and appeals to eco-conscious clients. Simple steps like recycling, reducing energy consumption, and using environmentally friendly cleaning products can make a difference. Investing in energy-efficient lighting and appliances, and encouraging carpooling or the use of public transportation among staff and students, can further reduce your studio's carbon footprint.

Implementing these practices can also be a great marketing point. Highlighting your commitment to sustainability in your promotional materials and communications can attract clients who prioritize eco-friendly practices. You can even incorporate themes of environmental consciousness into your dance programs, creating performances that raise awareness about important ecological issues.

Creating a culture of sustainability within your studio not only helps the environment but also fosters a sense of responsibility and community among staff and students. Encouraging everyone to participate in green initiatives, such as organizing clean-up drives or participating in local environmental campaigns, can strengthen community bonds and instill a sense of pride in being part of a forward-thinking and responsible organization.

Summary and Reflections

Understanding the financial aspects and business models in the dance industry is fundamental to building a successful dance studio or company. This chapter provided insights into creating a detailed business plan, covering revenue projections and expenses to ensure financial sustainability. We explored effective bookkeeping practices, the importance of identifying diverse funding sources, and the strategic setting of pricing structures. These elements are essential in maintaining a clear picture of your financial health and planning for future growth opportunities.

Operational efficiency and long-term sustainability were highlighted as key factors in thriving within the competitive dance industry. Utilizing management software for administrative tasks, developing a team of qualified instructors, and adopting green practices can enhance both efficiency and reputation. Engaging with the community and leveraging online marketing also play crucial roles in attracting and retaining clients. Implementing these strategies will not only help in managing day-to-day operations smoothly but also create a welcoming environment that encourages students and staff to be part of a thriving dance community.

Chapter 8:

Building Long-term Client Relationships

Building long-term client relationships in the dance industry is essential for a thriving and sustainable business. The foundation of these relationships is communication, which fosters trust and satisfaction between instructors and their clients. Young adults aspiring to build a career in dance, seasoned dance instructors, and event promoters alike will find that maintaining open dialogue and understanding client needs are key to achieving lasting success. Engaging with clients meaningfully not only makes them feel valued but also encourages repeat business and referrals, boosting one's reputation in the competitive dance world.

This chapter delves into effective communication techniques crucial for building and nurturing client relationships. You'll learn about active listening, a skill that goes beyond just hearing words to understanding the emotions and intentions behind them. Discover how tailoring services to meet individual client preferences can significantly enhance satisfaction. We'll explore strategies like reflective listening to demonstrate understanding and the importance of creating an environment where clients feel comfortable sharing feedback. By implementing these techniques, you'll be well-equipped to foster deep connections, create loyal clientele, and ensure continuous improvement in your dance business.

Effective Communication Techniques

Clear and effective communication is the cornerstone of building long-term client relationships in the dance industry. One of the most crucial skills to master in this regard is active listening. By genuinely understanding client needs and feedback, dance instructors and business owners can tailor their services to meet specific client preferences, create a sense of trust, and foster an environment where open dialogue leads to continuous improvement.

Active listening goes beyond just hearing words; it involves understanding the emotions and intentions behind those words. For young adults aspiring to build a career in dance, developing active listening skills means paying close attention when clients express their desires and concerns. For instance, if a client mentions struggling with a particular dance technique, acknowledging their struggle and asking follow-up questions shows that you are invested in their success. This approach not only helps in addressing immediate concerns but also provides invaluable insights into areas for potential growth and improvement.

It's not just about listening, though. It's equally important to demonstrate that you've understood what has been communicated. Reflective listening techniques, such as paraphrasing what the client has said or summarizing their key points, can assure them that you are on the same page. For example, after a client shares their goals for a dance event, summarizing by saying, "So, you're looking for a routine that emphasizes elegance and energy for the upcoming competition?" reinforces your comprehension and commitment to their vision. Tailoring services to meet specific client preferences is another vital aspect of maintaining strong client relationships. Each client will have unique tastes, needs, and expectations. By personalizing your approach, you show that you value their individuality. Whether it's adjusting a private lesson to focus more on specific dance moves or customizing choreography to suit a client's personal style, these small but meaningful adjustments can significantly enhance client satisfaction. A practical guideline here is always to keep a record of client preferences, such as favorite music genres or preferred teaching methods. This way, you can easily refer back and make each session more relevant and enjoyable for them.

Building trust through attentive listening ties everything together. Trust is earned when clients feel heard and understood. When dance instructors take the time to listen actively and respond thoughtfully, they convey respect and care, fostering deeper connections. Trust is not built overnight but through consistent and genuine interactions. An example could be following up on previous conversations, "How has practicing that new move we worked on last week gone?" Such questions indicate that you are invested in their progress and well-being, which strengthens the bond between instructor and client.

Creating an open dialogue for continuous improvement is essential for sustaining long-term relationships. Open dialogue encourages clients to share their thoughts freely, leading to collaborative solutions and enhancements. To cultivate an environment where clients feel comfortable sharing feedback, it is important to maintain a non-judgmental attitude and encourage honesty. For instance, periodically asking clients for their input on how classes or sessions can be improved demonstrates that their opinions matter and that you're willing to adapt for their benefit. Implementing simple feedback mechanisms like anonymous suggestion boxes or regular one-on-one check-ins can also facilitate more open communication.

Clear Instructional Communication

Providing guidance and feedback effectively is a crucial aspect of building long-term relationships in the dance industry. Whether you're a dance instructor aiming to expand your knowledge, a young adult pursuing an entrepreneurial career in dance, or an event promoter looking to host successful dance events, mastering the art of communication can set you apart. This section will delve into using language resonant with clients, clarifying complex dance techniques in relatable ways, offering constructive feedback, and ensuring comprehension through demonstrations and analogies.

To begin, using language that resonates with clients is foundational to effective communication. When interacting with clients, it's essential to understand their background, experience level, and preferences. For instance, using technical jargon with beginners may overwhelm them, whereas more experienced dancers might appreciate detailed terminology. Customize your language to match the client's familiarity with dance. If a client is new, explain movements in simple terms, perhaps even comparing them to everyday activities. For example, when teaching a basic pirouette, you could say, "Imagine you're screwing a light bulb with your body." This metaphor helps convey the concept in an easily understandable manner, making the learning process smoother and more enjoyable.

Equally important is clarifying complex dance techniques in a relatable manner. Dance is an art form that combines physical movement with emotion, and breaking down intricate steps can be challenging. One effective technique is to divide the movements into smaller, manageable sections. For instance, when teaching a complicated routine, start by focusing on the footwork before progressing to arm movements and expressions. Using visual aids such as diagrams or videos can also enhance understanding. Another strategy is storytelling. Narrating a story that aligns with the dance can create a mental picture for the dancer, aiding in grasping both the technique and the emotional expression required. If a dance sequence represents a journey, describe each phase of the journey in correlation with the movements, allowing dancers to connect emotionally and physically with the routine.

Offering constructive feedback is another vital component that fosters growth. It's important to deliver feedback in a way that motivates rather than discourages. Begin by highlighting what the client did well before addressing areas for improvement. This technique, often referred to as the "praise-critique-praise" method, ensures that the client remains positive and receptive. For example, if a dancer performed a sequence with excellent rhythm but struggled with alignment, you could say, "Your timing was spot on; it really brought the energy to life. Now, let's focus on your posture to make those moves even sharper." Additionally, frame feedback as opportunities for growth rather than failures. Acknowledge the effort and progress, emphasizing that perfection comes with practice and perseverance. Encouraging self-reflection by asking questions like, "How did that feel to you?" can also empower clients to assess their performance and identify areas for improvement independently.

Ensuring comprehension through demonstrations and analogies is equally essential. Visual and kinesthetic learners benefit greatly from seeing and experiencing movements firsthand. Demonstrate the steps yourself or use advanced students as models, breaking down each movement and explaining the nuances. Encourage clients to mirror your actions, providing immediate corrections and adjustments. Analogies are powerful tools in this context as well. Comparing a dance move to a familiar action can simplify complex techniques. For instance, when teaching a glide step, liken it to "ice skating on a smooth surface," which evokes the sense of effortless motion. Additionally, employing hands-on adjustments can provide real-time feedback. With permission, gently guide the client's limbs to the correct position, allowing them to feel the proper alignment and muscle engagement.

Prompt and Professional Responses

Enhancing customer experience through timely communication is fundamental in building long-term client relationships, especially in the dance industry. When clients feel heard and valued, they are more likely to remain loyal and recommend your services to others. One critical aspect of enhancing customer experience is responding to queries or concerns promptly.

In today's fast-paced world, people expect quick responses to their inquiries. Whether it's a potential client reaching out for information about classes or an existing student with a concern, timely communication shows that you value their time and are dedicated to meeting their needs. Set a standard response time for all communications—whether via email, social media, or phone—and strive to adhere to it consistently. For instance, aim to respond to all emails within 24 hours and all social media messages within a few hours during business days. This simple guideline can go a long way in establishing trust and reliability.

Equally important is maintaining professionalism across all communication channels. Professionalism doesn't mean being overly formal; rather, it means being respectful, clear, and consistent in your messaging. Always address clients by their names, express gratitude for their interest or feedback, and provide thoughtful and thorough answers. For example, if a parent emails to inquire about a dance class for their child, a professional response would include a warm greeting, detailed information about the class, and a closing remark expressing enthusiasm about the potential of seeing their child in class. Avoid using jargon or slang that might confuse or alienate your audience. Instead, keep your language simple and clear.

Follow-ups are another crucial element in ensuring client satisfaction. After an initial interaction, don't let the conversation end there. Implement follow-up practices to check in on how the client is doing and whether their needs have been met. If someone signs up for a class, send a quick message after the first session to ask how they enjoyed it and if they have any questions. Similarly, if a client expresses dissatisfaction, follow up after addressing their concern to ensure they are satisfied with the resolution. These small gestures show that you care about their experience and are committed to continuous improvement.

Utilizing multiple communication platforms is also essential for accessibility. Different clients may prefer different methods of communication—some may like emails, while others might prefer texts, phone calls, or social media messages. By being present on various platforms, you make it easier for clients to reach you in a way that's convenient for them. For example, while older clients might prefer phone calls or emails, younger clients might be more comfortable with texting or messaging through social media apps. Make sure you regularly monitor and respond to messages on all these platforms to ensure no client feels ignored or undervalued.

Timely and effective communication can also enhance the overall customer experience by resolving any issues before they escalate. For instance, if a student can't attend a class and informs you ahead of time, a prompt response allowing them to reschedule demonstrates flexibility and understanding. This not only addresses the immediate concern but also builds goodwill and loyalty. Moreover, providing regular updates about upcoming events, class schedules, and any changes ensures that clients are always informed and engaged.

Using a blend of proactive and reactive strategies can further strengthen your communication efforts. Proactively, send regular newsletters or updates to keep your clients informed about new classes, events, or important announcements. This keeps your clients engaged and excited about what's coming next. Reactively, always be ready to address any unexpected issues or questions as they arise. For instance, if there's a sudden change in class schedule due to unforeseen circumstances, inform your clients immediately with clear instructions on the next steps.

Another key aspect of enhancing customer experience through communication is personalizing your interactions. Take note of clients' preferences, birthdays, and milestones. A quick birthday message or a note congratulating a student on their progress can make a significant impact. Personal touches show that you see your clients as individuals and appreciate their unique contributions to your community.

Lastly, consider implementing a feedback loop. Encourage clients to share their thoughts and experiences regularly. Whether through surveys, suggestion boxes, or casual conversations, gathering feedback gives you insight into areas where you can improve and also reinforces that you value their opinions. Addressing feedback promptly and transparently can turn even negative experiences into positive outcomes.

Concluding Thoughts

Building and maintaining a loyal client base in the dance industry relies heavily on effective communication. Throughout this chapter, we explored how active listening, reflective techniques, and personalized services play a critical role. By genuinely understanding client needs and demonstrating that you have grasped their concerns, you create trust and foster deeper connections. Tailoring services to individual preferences not only enhances satisfaction but also shows clients that they are valued. These practices, combined with continuous improvements based on open dialogue, ensure that clients feel heard and appreciated.

Additionally, prompt and professional responses are essential in nurturing long-term relationships. Quick replies to inquiries and thoughtful follow-ups show that you are committed to your clients' experience. Utilizing multiple communication platforms caters to different client preferences, making it easier for them to reach out. Personal touches, like remembering milestones and offering regular updates, further reinforce the sense of individual attention. By consistently applying these communication strategies, you can build a strong, loyal client base that feels supported and respected, paving the way for sustained success in the dance industry.

Chapter 9:

Dance Instructors: Independent vs. Collaborative

Dance instructors often find themselves navigating between the appeal of independence and the benefits of collaboration. The choice to work independently or within a studio framework significantly impacts their professional journey, influencing everything from teaching styles to business operations. For many, this decision shapes not only how they interact with students but also how they manage their time, finances, and career growth. Understanding these dynamics provides valuable insights into the dance community's diverse landscape and allows aspiring instructors to make informed choices about their career paths. In this chapter, we'll explore the intricacies of both independent and collaborative work among dance instructors. We'll delve into the freedoms and challenges that come with running a solo practice, such as developing unique teaching methodologies and managing business logistics. Conversely, we'll discuss the supportive environment that collaborations can offer, highlighting shared resources, networking opportunities, and collective problem-solving. By examining these two approaches, we aim to understand how dance instructors can use studio spaces effectively and foster a thriving career in the world of dance.

Independent Dance Instructors

Understanding Independent Dance Instructors
Let's dive into understanding the life of an independent dance instructor. These dedicated professionals possess a unique blend of passion for dance and entrepreneurial spirit, forming a world where creativity meets business. They have the autonomy to design their own schedules,

curriculum, and teaching styles, which can be both liberating and challenging.

One of the most significant advantages of working independently is the freedom to run one's own business. This autonomy allows instructors to make decisions that align with their vision and teaching philosophy. For example, they can choose the types of dance they want to specialize in, select venues that best suit their needs, and decide on the demographic they wish to target. This level of control can lead to increased job satisfaction as instructors are able to express their creativity without constraints. Furthermore, they do not have to conform to pre-established systems or methodologies imposed by others, which can sometimes stifle individual expression.

However, with great power comes great responsibility. Independent dance instructors face numerous challenges that can be daunting for those new to the field. Marketing is one such challenge. Unlike instructors working within a studio, independents must actively promote themselves to attract clients. This involves creating engaging social media content, developing a professional website, and utilizing word-of-mouth recommendations. Networking at dance events and workshops also becomes crucial as it helps in establishing connections that can lead to referrals and new opportunities.

Scheduling classes is another aspect that requires careful consideration. Instructors need to be adept at time management to balance multiple classes, private lessons, and personal practice sessions. Conflicts are bound to arise, and being able to resolve them efficiently is essential to maintain a steady workflow and client satisfaction. Additionally, managing cancellations and rescheduling can add another layer of complexity.

Client management is equally important. Building strong relationships with students fosters loyalty and encourages repeat business. This involves understanding each student's needs, providing constructive feedback, and creating a supportive learning environment. Clear communication is key; setting expectations regarding class rules, payment policies, and progress tracking helps avoid misunderstandings and ensures smooth operations.

Financial aspects form the backbone of any independent venture. Setting rates for classes and private lessons requires a fine balance between competitiveness and profitability.

Dance Teaching Business

Instructors need to research market trends, evaluate their own skill level and experience, and consider the economic landscape of their location. Rates should reflect the value offered, ensuring they are neither too low (which might undermine perceived quality) nor too high (which could deter potential clients).

Handling taxes and managing expenses are inevitable parts of running a business. Instructors must stay organized, keeping track of income and expenditures meticulously. Investing in accounting software or consulting with a financial advisor can simplify this process. Expenses can include studio rental fees, marketing costs, travel, costumes, and music licensing, among others. Keeping detailed records helps in budgeting effectively and preparing for tax obligations, which can vary significantly based on local laws and regulations. Additionally, building a personal brand is critical in the dance industry. Your brand is more than just your name; it encompasses your reputation, teaching style, and the overall experience you provide to your clients. A strong brand can set you apart from competitors and attract students who resonate with your approach. Social media platforms like Instagram, Facebook, and

YouTube offer powerful tools for showcasing your work, sharing testimonials, and connecting with a broader audience. Regularly updating these channels with high-quality content keeps you relevant and accessible.

Moreover, attending industry events, conferences, and competitions enhances visibility and credibility. These occasions provide invaluable opportunities for networking with peers and potential clients, staying updated on industry trends, and gaining inspiration from other professionals. Participating in or hosting workshops and masterclasses not only boosts skills but also establishes the instructor as a thought leader in the dance community.

Collaborative Dance Instructors

Exploring the benefits and procedures of collaborative work for dance instructors allows us to understand how teamwork can enhance creativity, foster growth, and provide a support system in the competitive world of dance.

Working within an established studio and utilizing shared resources is often the first step for many dance instructors looking to collaborate. Established studios usually have well-maintained facilities that come equipped with mirrors, sound systems, and sometimes even sprung floors designed to reduce injury risks. Utilizing these shared resources not only saves costs but also ensures that instructors can offer high-quality classes to their students. In addition, many studios offer marketing and administrative support, allowing instructors to focus more on teaching rather than operational logistics. This mutually beneficial arrangement can help both the instructor and the studio grow their clientele.

Navigating agreements and contracts with studio owners is crucial for a smooth collaboration. Before starting, it's essential to have a clear contract that outlines each party's responsibilities, the terms of studio usage, and financial arrangements, such as rental fees or revenue-sharing models. Being upfront about expectations and getting everything in writing helps prevent misunderstandings down the line. Contracts should also specify scheduling details, ensuring that studio space is efficiently allocated and conflicts are minimized. For example, if an instructor offers contemporary dance classes while another focuses on ballroom dancing, careful scheduling can ensure that each class gets appropriate time and space without overlap. Balancing creative input while maintaining individual teaching styles is another key aspect of successful collaboration. Every dance instructor has a unique approach and philosophy towards dance education. When working collaboratively, it's important to respect each other's creative processes and find a balance that allows for individual expression within a cohesive framework. Regular meetings and open communication channels can facilitate this balance, providing opportunities for instructors to share their ideas and receive feedback from peers. This not only enriches the learning experience for students but also encourages professional growth among instructors.

One of the significant benefits of collaborative work includes mutual support among instructors. Teaching dance can be physically and emotionally demanding, so having a team to lean on during challenging times makes a big difference. Instructors can share tips, encourage one another, and provide constructive feedback, creating a nurturing environment that promotes overall well-being. Mutual support extends beyond day-to-day teaching; it can also involve covering each other's classes during absences or emergencies, ensuring that students' learning remains uninterrupted.

Networking opportunities are another advantage of working collaboratively. Connecting with fellow instructors, studio owners, and even students opens doors to new prospects, such as guest teaching spots, workshops, or performance gigs. These connections can prove invaluable when looking to expand one's career or business. Collaborative environments naturally create networking spaces where sharing knowledge and experience builds stronger professional relationships. For instance, participating in studio-hosted events or joint performances can showcase an instructor's skills to a wider audience, leading to greater recognition and opportunities within the dance community.

Shared responsibilities are a practical benefit of collaborative work. Running a dance studio involves numerous tasks beyond teaching, such as marketing, billing, and maintaining the facilities. By collaborating, instructors can distribute these responsibilities more equitably, preventing burnout and allowing them to focus on their strengths. For example, one instructor might handle social media promotions due to their tech-savviness, while another might oversee costume management for recitals because of their organizational skills. This division of labor ensures that all aspects of the studio run smoothly without placing undue burden on any single person.

Moreover, collaborative work fosters a culture of continuous improvement. Instructors regularly interacting and observing each other's classes can inspire new teaching techniques or choreography ideas. Constructive feedback sessions allow for reflection and refinement, pushing everyone to elevate their standards. This culture of ongoing learning and adaptation is particularly beneficial in the ever-evolving field of dance, where trends and styles constantly change.

In practice, collaborative work requires setting clear boundaries and guidelines. Using someone else's premises or studio space to conduct business necessitates adherence to specific procedures and responsibilities. It's essential to respect the studio's rules and maintain a professional demeanor at all times. Instructors should aim to leave the space as they found it, ensuring that equipment is put away properly and the studio remains clean and inviting for the next user. Meeting these shared responsibilities upholds the integrity of the studio and fosters a respectful, cooperative environment.

Appropriate procedure and responsibilities also extend to interactions with students and fellow instructors. Establishing a code of conduct that outlines expected behaviors can help maintain a positive atmosphere. Open communication and mutual respect should be cornerstones of any collaborative endeavor, ensuring that conflicts are handled constructively, and everyone feels valued and heard.

Insights and Implications

In this chapter, we've delved into the dynamic world of dance instruction, examining both independent and collaborative approaches. Independent instructors enjoy the freedom to shape their own schedules, teaching styles, and business strategies, which allows for unparalleled creativity and personal fulfillment. However, they also face significant challenges, such as marketing themselves, managing finances, and juggling multiple responsibilities. On the other hand, collaborative work within established studios offers numerous benefits, including shared resources, networking opportunities, and mutual support among instructors. While it requires navigating contracts and balancing individual teaching styles, working together can lead to a more enriching and sustainable career in dance.

By exploring these two distinct paths, we aimed to provide a comprehensive understanding of what it takes to thrive as a dance instructor. Whether you're just starting out or looking to expand your business, the insights shared here highlight the importance of adaptability, clear communication, and continuous improvement. Embracing either an independent or collaborative approach—or even combining elements of both—can help you build a successful and fulfilling career. Remember, the key is to align your professional choices with your personal vision and goals, always staying committed to your passion for dance.

PART 4:

DANCE In The Commercial Field

Chapter 10:

Adapting to Technological Changes

Adapting to technological changes is essential for anyone looking to build a successful dance career. In today's digital age, technology offers new ways to learn, teach, and connect within the dance community. By embracing these advancements, dancers and instructors can enhance their skills, broaden their reach, and create vibrant, collaborative networks. From online classes to innovative interactive tools, technology presents numerous opportunities that were once unimaginable.

This chapter delves into how you can incorporate various technological elements into your dance career. You will explore the benefits of online classes and workshops, which allow dancers to learn from global talent without leaving home. We'll also discuss the convenience and flexibility offered by virtual platforms, making it easier to practice and improve at your own pace. Additionally, we'll examine interactive learning tools that provide personalized feedback and help refine your techniques. Whether you are an aspiring dancer, an instructor, or an event promoter, this chapter will guide you on how to leverage technology to elevate your dance journey.

Online Classes and Workshops

In today's fast-paced digital world, dancers and dance instructors have access to a plethora of online platforms that can significantly enhance their education and skill set. These platforms are instrumental in providing opportunities for dancers to connect with global talent, practice at their convenience, and utilize interactive learning tools tailored to their needs.

One of the most significant benefits of online platforms is the ability to access global talent. Traditionally, dancers were limited to learning from local instructors or traveling to different cities and countries to attend workshops and classes. With the advent of online platforms, this barrier has been removed. Dancers can now take classes from renowned instructors worldwide without leaving their homes. For instance, a dancer in New York can easily enroll in a flamenco class taught by a master in Spain. This accessibility not only broadens the range of dance styles available to learners but also exposes them to various teaching methods and cultural interpretations of dance.

Moreover, connecting with global talent fosters a sense of community and collaboration among dancers. Online forums, social media groups, and virtual meet-ups create spaces where dancers can share experiences, seek advice, and support each other's growth. This global network is invaluable, especially for those aspiring to build a career in dance. It opens doors to potential collaborations, mentorships, and even job opportunities across different parts of the world. Aspiring dancers can benefit tremendously from the diverse perspectives and insights they gain through these interactions, enriching their personal and professional development.

Another key advantage of online dance platforms is the convenience and flexibility they offer. Traditional dance classes often require strict adherence to schedules, which may not be feasible for everyone. Online platforms, however, allow dancers to learn at their own pace and on their schedule. Whether you're a full-time student, a working professional, or someone juggling multiple responsibilities, you can fit dance practice into your routine whenever it suits you best.

Guideline: To make the most of this flexibility, it's essential to set specific goals and create a structured practice schedule. Allocate dedicated time slots for lessons, practice, and review sessions to ensure consistent progress. Additionally, taking advantage of recorded classes allows you to revisit complex techniques and refine your skills as needed.

The convenience of practicing at home also eliminates the need for commuting, saving both time and money. This is particularly beneficial for those living in remote areas with limited access to high-quality dance instruction. By removing geographical constraints, online platforms democratize dance education, making it accessible to a broader audience.

Interactive learning tools are another feature of online platforms that revolutionize dance education. These tools can provide an engaging and personalized learning experience, catering to the unique needs of each dancer. For example, some platforms use video conferencing to offer live classes, where instructors can observe students' movements in real time and provide immediate feedback. This interaction closely mimics the experience of in-studio classes, ensuring that dancers receive the guidance and corrections necessary for improvement.

Guideline: During live classes, position your camera to accurately capture your full body movements. Ensure you have a stable internet connection to avoid disruptions. Actively engage with your instructor, asking questions and seeking clarification when needed. This proactive approach will help you make the most of the interactive features and improve your learning outcomes.

Additionally, many online platforms incorporate various multimedia elements to enhance the learning process. Interactive tutorials, step-by-step breakdowns of choreography, and practice drills are just a few examples. These resources allow dancers to learn new moves and techniques methodically, reinforcing their understanding through repetition and visual aids. Some platforms also offer quizzes and assessments to track progress, helping dancers identify areas for improvement.

For dance instructors, online platforms present an opportunity to expand their reach and grow their business. By offering virtual classes, instructors can attract students from all over the world, transcending the limitations of physical studio space. This expanded audience can lead to increased revenue and greater brand recognition in the dance community. Furthermore, online platforms often provide tools for managing class schedules, payments, and student communication, streamlining administrative tasks and allowing instructors to focus more on teaching.

Event promoters can also benefit from utilizing online platforms for hosting dance events. Virtual workshops, competitions, and showcases can reach a wider audience, attracting participants and spectators from different regions. These online events can serve as valuable networking opportunities, bringing together dancers, instructors, and industry professionals. Promoters can leverage the power of social media and online marketing to increase visibility and engagement for their events, creating a vibrant and inclusive dance community.

Online platforms for dance education and skill enhancement offer numerous benefits, from accessing global talent and enjoying convenience and flexibility to utilizing interactive learning tools. These platforms empower dancers to learn from the best instructors worldwide, practice at their own pace, and engage with innovative educational resources. By embracing these opportunities, dancers, instructors, and event promoters alike can elevate their craft and thrive in the ever-evolving landscape of dance.

Interactive Learning Tools

Utilizing virtual platforms for engaging and tailored dance instruction opens up a wealth of opportunities for dancers at any stage of their career. These platforms offer innovative methods to receive feedback, improve skills, and fine-tune performance in ways that were not possible before.

One of the most significant advantages of these virtual tools is the ability to receive live feedback from instructors through video conferencing. This real-time interaction provides immediate corrections and guidance on technique, form, and expression. For instance, during a virtual ballet class, an instructor can spot a dancer's alignment issue or incorrect execution of a movement and give instant advice to rectify it. This level of engagement ensures that dancers do not develop bad habits over time, which can be harder to correct later. It also mimics the traditional classroom experience, maintaining a sense of connection between teacher and student despite the physical distance.

Moreover, the availability of on-demand content has revolutionized how dancers practice and learn. Online libraries filled with recorded classes allow dancers to revisit lessons as many times as needed, making it easier to master challenging routines or techniques. This resource is invaluable for those who may need more time to understand specific instructions or wish to perfect a particular sequence. The flexibility to access these classes at any time fits seamlessly into a dancer's schedule, accommodating those who juggle multiple commitments, such as school or work.

In addition to real-time and on-demand options, advanced technology like motion capture and AI plays a crucial role in enhancing dance instruction. Motion capture technology records a dancer's movements in detail, allowing for a thorough analysis of their performance. This data can highlight areas for improvement that might be missed even by trained eyes. For example, subtle deviations in posture or limb positioning can be identified and addressed, helping the dancer achieve a higher level of precision.

AI takes this one step further by providing personalized feedback tailored to each dancer's specific needs. By analyzing the captured data, AI can generate customized training programs that target weaknesses and build on strengths. Imagine a tap dancer using AI technology to perfect their timing and rhythm. The system could detect slight inconsistencies and suggest exercises to refine their technique, making their performance tighter and more polished.

The integration of these technologies does more than just improve individual skills. It democratizes access to high-quality dance education. Dancers who might not have proximity to seasoned instructors or prestigious schools can now receive top-notch training from anywhere in the world. This broadens the reach of dance education, ensuring that talent is nurtured regardless of geographical constraints.

Virtual platforms also foster a collaborative learning environment. Community features such as forums, group chats, and social media integrations encourage dancers to share progress, pose questions, and support one another. This sense of community can be especially motivating and help maintain a dancer's enthusiasm. For example, sharing a video of a recently learned routine and receiving constructive feedback from peers or instructors can provide valuable insights and encouragement to keep improving.

Another advantage of utilizing these virtual tools is their cost-effectiveness. Traditional dance classes often come with expenses related to commuting, facility rentals, and other overheads. Virtual classes eliminate many of these costs, making high-quality dance instruction more affordable and accessible. This financial aspect is particularly appealing to young adults aspiring to build a dance career with limited resources. They can invest wisely in their training without compromising on quality.

Moreover, these platforms often incorporate interactive elements that enhance learning. Features like quizzes, progress trackers, and goal-setting modules keep dancers engaged and motivated. For instance, a platform might offer a series of progressively challenging tasks to complete within a set timeframe, rewarding achievements with badges or certificates. This gamification adds a fun and competitive edge to learning, making the process enjoyable while reinforcing commitment to practice.

Real-time feedback capabilities are instrumental in creating a dynamic learning experience. Unlike pre-recorded videos, live sessions allow for spontaneous adjustments and personalized attention. An instructor can adapt the pace of the class based on the dancers' performance, spend more time on difficult sections, or introduce variations to challenge more advanced students. This adaptability ensures that each session meets the participants' needs, maximizing the effectiveness of the practice.

Lastly, the incorporation of advanced technology and adaptive learning tools in virtual platforms extends beyond just technical improvements. It also fosters creativity, as dancers are encouraged to experiment with new styles and approaches. For example, motion capture data might reveal an innovative way to execute a spin or jump, sparking fresh ideas and creative exploration. This blend of technology and artistry enriches the overall dance experience.

Final Thoughts

Embracing technology in your dance career opens a world of possibilities. Online platforms allow dancers to connect with renowned instructors globally, enriching their learning experience without leaving home. This ease of access helps dancers explore various styles and techniques, fostering personal growth and professional development. The ability to learn at your own pace adds flexibility, making it easier to balance dance with other commitments. Moreover, the interactive tools available on these platforms ensure that you receive immediate feedback and tailored guidance, closely replicating the traditional in-studio experience.

For instructors and event promoters, these online tools offer an opportunity to reach wider audiences and enhance their business. Virtual classes can attract students from different regions, creating a diverse learning environment. Online events and workshops can unite dancers, instructors, and enthusiasts worldwide, forming a vibrant community. By leveraging these technological advancements, you not only elevate your skills but also contribute to a more inclusive and connected dance world. Embrace these platforms to transform your passion into a thriving career and make dance education accessible to everyone, everywhere.

Chapter 11:

Maintaining Physical and Mental Well-being

Maintaining physical and mental well-being is essential for dancers striving to sustain long and prosperous careers. In this chapter, we delve into strategies and practices that underscore the importance of overall wellness. From physical conditioning to injury prevention, we explore a variety of techniques that can help dancers enhance their strength, flexibility, and resilience. Regular conditioning regimes play a vital role in minimizing the risk of injuries, which can significantly disrupt or cut short a dancer's career. Additionally, proper warm-up and cool-down routines are highlighted as critical components for preparing the body for strenuous activities and aiding recovery post-performance. We also examine the benefits of incorporating cross-training activities such as swimming and yoga to prevent overuse injuries and improve overall fitness. Adequate rest and recovery periods are essential to avoid burnout and chronic injuries, emphasizing the necessity of sleep and light activities during rest days. The chapter further discusses the crucial roles of hydration and nutrition in maintaining peak physical health. For young aspiring dancers, cultivating good habits early on regarding physical conditioning, nutrition, and rest are keys to longevity and performance enhancement. Dance instructors and event promoters are encouraged to stress these points, teaching by example and fostering comprehensive health education among their students and participants.

Physical Conditioning and Injury Prevention

Maintaining physical health is crucial for dancers who aim to sustain long and successful careers. Regular physical conditioning plays an essential role in this process. By consistently working on strength and flexibility, dancers can significantly reduce the risk of injuries that might otherwise interrupt or even end their careers. Conditioning isn't just about intense workouts; it involves a balanced regimen that targets all muscle groups, ensuring that they are not only strong but also flexible and resilient.

One key aspect of maintaining physical health is having proper warm-up and cool-down routines. Warm-ups prepare the muscles and joints for the strenuous activity ahead. Starting with light cardio exercises like jogging or skipping can elevate the heart rate gradually, increasing blood flow to the muscles. This, combined with dynamic stretches that mimic the movements dancers will perform, ensures that the body is ready to handle the physical demands of dancing. Conversely, cooling down after a session is equally important. It helps bring the heart rate back to normal and prevents stiffness by removing lactic acid build-up in the muscles. Gentle stretching and low-intensity activities such as walking can facilitate recovery and reduce the likelihood of muscle strains and joint issues.

To prevent overuse injuries, incorporating cross-training activities into the routine is highly recommended. Cross-training involves engaging in different types of exercise to work various muscle groups and improve overall fitness. Activities like swimming or yoga are excellent options. Swimming provides a full-body workout without putting excessive strain on the joints, making it ideal for enhancing cardiovascular endurance and strength. Yoga, on the other hand, focuses on flexibility, balance, and mental clarity. The practice of different poses and controlled breathing in yoga complements dance training by promoting muscle elongation and relaxation, reducing the risk of injuries due to tightness and imbalances.

Adequate rest and recovery time are also vital components of a dancer's physical health strategy. Dancing extensively without allowing sufficient recovery periods can lead to burnout and chronic injuries. Rest days give the body's systems, including the muscles, tendons, and ligaments, time to repair and strengthen. During these periods, engaging in light activities like walking or gentle stretching can help maintain mobility without exerting too much stress on the body. Sleeping enough each night is another critical factor; quality sleep enables the body to undergo vital repair processes, supporting overall health and well-being.

In addition to the aforementioned strategies, hydration and nutrition play significant roles in a dancer's physical maintenance. Staying hydrated ensures that the muscles remain supple and reduces the risk of cramps. Drinking water throughout the day, not just during practice sessions, keeps the body functioning optimally. Likewise, a well-balanced diet rich in proteins, carbohydrates, healthy fats, vitamins, and minerals supports energy levels and muscle repair. Consuming meals and snacks at regular intervals helps maintain stable energy levels, which is particularly important for dancers who typically have demanding schedules.

Understanding the importance of these elements and integrating them into daily routines requires discipline and commitment. For young aspiring dancers, starting early to develop good habits around physical conditioning, warming up, cooling down, cross-training, rest, hydration, and nutrition is crucial. These practices will not only enhance performance but also ensure longevity in their dance careers. Dance instructors and event promoters should also emphasize these points to their students and participants. Instructors can lead by example, demonstrating effective warm-up techniques, suggesting diverse cross-training activities, and discussing the importance of rest and nutrition.

Mental Well-being and Stress Management

Ensuring overall wellness to sustain a long career in dance is critical for both mental and physical health. Let's delve into some powerful techniques for managing performance anxiety and coping with stage fright through mindfulness and relaxation exercises.

Performance anxiety can be an overwhelming experience, especially when stepping onto the stage. To manage this, dancers can practice mindfulness. Mindfulness involves focusing on the present moment without judgment. This allows dancers to center themselves, reducing anxiety levels. One effective method is deep breathing exercises. Before a performance, taking a few minutes to breathe deeply and slowly can significantly calm the nerves. Additionally, progressive muscle relaxation, which involves tensing and then slowly releasing each muscle group, helps release built-up tension within the body.

Another useful technique is visualization. Imagine yourself performing flawlessly, with confidence and grace. This positive imagery not only boosts self-confidence but also creates a mental rehearsal that prepares you for the actual performance. Combined with positive affirmations such as "I am prepared" or "I am confident," these exercises can effectively diminish the fear of failure and enhance overall performance quality.

Establishing a robust support network is equally vital. A strong backing of mentors, peers, and mental health professionals provides emotional resilience. Mentors offer guidance and share their own experiences, helping dancers navigate through tough times. They can provide advice on honing skills, overcoming obstacles, and maintaining passion for dance. Connecting with fellow dancers who understand the unique pressures can also create a sense of camaraderie and mutual support.

For more personalized assistance, consulting mental health professionals can be immensely beneficial. These experts can provide strategies tailored to individual needs, helping dancers manage stress, anxiety, and other emotional challenges. Having a trusted professional to talk to can make a significant difference in maintaining mental well-being and ensuring longevity in one's dance career.

Furthermore, developing healthy lifestyle habits plays a crucial role in supporting cognitive function. Consuming a balanced diet rich in nutrients fuels the body and brain. Proper nutrition ensures that dancers have the energy needed for practice and performance while maintaining overall health. Foods high in omega-3 fatty acids, antioxidants, and vitamins are particularly beneficial for brain function and mental clarity. Hydration is also essential; keeping hydrated enhances concentration and reduces fatigue.

Adequate sleep is another cornerstone of cognitive support. The importance of a good night's sleep cannot be overstated. During sleep, the brain processes new information, repairs itself, and recharges. For dancers, proper rest ensures they can perform at their best, both mentally and physically. Establishing a consistent sleep routine, creating a relaxing bedtime environment, and avoiding caffeine or heavy meals before bed can promote better sleep quality.

Utilizing goal-setting and time management strategies is key to reducing stress and maintaining a healthy work-life balance. Setting clear, achievable goals helps dancers stay focused and motivated. Breaking down larger goals into smaller, manageable tasks makes them less daunting and more attainable. This structured approach prevents feelings of being overwhelmed and provides a clear path forward.

Time management is equally important. Efficiently organizing rehearsals, performances, and personal time ensures that dancers do not overextend themselves. Using tools like planners or digital calendars can help keep track of schedules and deadlines. It's also crucial to carve out time for relaxation and hobbies outside of dance. Engaging in activities you enjoy can rejuvenate your mind and body, providing a well-rounded life experience.

Summary and Reflections

Embracing overall wellness is an essential part of sustaining a long and fulfilling dance career. By focusing on both physical and mental health, dancers can enhance their performance while preventing injuries and burnout. Physical conditioning through balanced workouts, proper warm-ups, cool-down routines, cross-training, adequate rest, hydration, and nutrition creates a strong foundation for success. Equally important is managing stress and performance anxiety with mindfulness techniques, building a support network, and fostering healthy lifestyle habits. These practices help maintain mental clarity and emotional resilience, allowing dancers to navigate the challenges of their demanding profession.

Incorporating these wellness practices into daily routines requires dedication but yields significant rewards. For young aspiring dancers, starting early with these habits not only enhances their immediate performance but also sets them up for long-term success. Dance instructors and event promoters can play a crucial role by emphasizing the importance of holistic wellness to their students and participants. By modeling effective techniques and promoting a balanced approach to training, they help create a supportive environment where dancers can thrive. Ensuring overall wellness is not just a strategy—it's a commitment to a sustainable and joyful dance career.

Chapter 12:

Inspiring Through Dance

Using dance as a medium for inspiration and change is a powerful concept that has the potential to transform individuals and communities. Through the universal language of movement, dance breaks down barriers and fosters connections between people from diverse backgrounds. It is in this shared experience that participants find common ground, empathy, and understanding, transcending cultural and social boundaries. This chapter delves into the myriad ways dance can serve as a catalyst for positive change, illustrating how it brings people together in creative and meaningful ways.

In the pages ahead, you will discover the various initiatives and programs that utilize dance to build stronger, more cohesive communities. From inclusive workshops that welcome both able-bodied dancers and those with disabilities to public performances that democratize access to the arts, each example highlights the transformative power of dance. You will also learn about the significant impact community dance programs have on underserved areas, providing accessible artistic outlets and fostering local pride and engagement. As the chapter unfolds, it will become clear how dance not only entertains but also unites, educates, and inspires, offering a unique pathway for social cohesion and personal growth.

Community Outreach and Engagement

Dance is a universal language that transcends cultural and social boundaries. When people come together to dance, they embark on a shared journey of movement, rhythm, and expression. This powerful medium has the potential to unite individuals and communities, fostering positive change through connection and understanding.

One way dance achieves this is through initiatives and workshops designed to bridge gaps between diverse groups. These programs provide a shared activity that encourages inclusion and interaction, allowing people from different backgrounds to come together in a space of mutual respect and creativity. For instance, a dance workshop that includes both able-bodied dancers and those with disabilities can promote empathy and inclusivity. By working side by side, participants learn to appreciate each other's unique contributions, breaking down barriers and building stronger, more cohesive communities.

Community dance programs are particularly impactful when they target underserved areas. In neighborhoods where resources for cultural activities may be limited, these programs offer an accessible means of artistic expression and a creative outlet for residents. For example, a community center in an economically disadvantaged area might host weekly dance classes for local youth. These classes not only provide a fun and healthy activity but also instill a sense of pride and accomplishment in the participants. When young people have the opportunity to engage in such enriching activities, they are more likely to stay engaged in their community and take on leadership roles, thereby contributing positively to their environment.

Collaborative dance events play a crucial role in generating a sense of belonging and unity. These events, often held in public spaces, invite members of the community to participate in or simply enjoy a shared cultural experience. Whether it's a flash mob in a city square or a choreographed piece performed at a local festival, these events encourage people to connect with one another in meaningful ways. The process of preparing for a collaborative dance event often involves teamwork, communication, and mutual support, which helps to strengthen neighborhood ties and reduce social isolation. As people work together towards a common goal, they form bonds that transcend the immediate context of the dance, fostering long-term relationships and a deeper sense of community.

Public dance performances are another effective way to bring art to local settings and make cultural experiences more inclusive. By staging performances in parks, streets, or other community spaces, dance becomes accessible to a wider audience, including those who might not typically attend a theater or dance studio. These performances can inspire, entertain, and educate, offering viewers a glimpse into different styles and traditions of dance. For instance, a public performance of traditional dances from various cultures can highlight the richness of diversity within a community, promoting mutual respect and understanding. Moreover, such events often draw in families and individuals from all walks of life, creating opportunities for intergenerational and intercultural connections.

In addition to fostering interpersonal connections, dance programs and events can also contribute to the economic and cultural vitality of a community. Festivals and performances can attract tourists, boosting local businesses and generating revenue. This, in turn, can lead to further investment in arts and culture, creating a positive feedback loop that benefits everyone involved. A vibrant dance scene can become a point of pride for a community, enhancing its reputation and drawing even more interest and engagement.

Ultimately, the power of dance lies in its ability to create moments of joy, connection, and transformation. When individuals come together to move as one, they experience a profound sense of belonging and shared purpose. This sense of unity can ripple outwards, influencing attitudes and behaviors beyond the dance floor. By participating in and supporting dance initiatives, communities can harness this power to foster positive change, building a more inclusive and harmonious world for all.

Dance initiatives and workshops serve as a crucial entry point for many individuals, offering them a chance to explore new forms of movement and expression. For example, a multicultural dance workshop can introduce participants to diverse dance styles, opening their minds to different cultural perspectives. These workshops often include discussions and reflections that help deepen understanding and appreciation among participants. By providing a safe and supportive environment, such initiatives enable individuals to step out of their comfort zones and engage with others in meaningful ways.

Community dance programs hold immense value, especially in areas where artistic opportunities are scarce. Programs like these often rely on dedicated volunteers and supporters who believe in the transformative power of dance. They can be particularly effective in engaging young people who might otherwise lack access to extracurricular activities. Through dance, these youths find a constructive outlet for their energy and emotions, helping them navigate the challenges of adolescence. Additionally, community dance programs often emphasize values such as discipline, perseverance, and teamwork, which are essential for personal growth and development.

Collaborative dance events often culminate in public performances that celebrate the collective effort of the participants. These events can range from small, intimate gatherings to large-scale productions involving hundreds of dancers. Regardless of the scale, the impact on the community is substantial. Participants feel a sense of accomplishment and pride in their contribution, while audiences experience the joy and inspiration that comes from witnessing a unified display of talent and creativity. Such events can leave a lasting impression, encouraging more people to get involved in future dance projects.

Public dance performances also play a significant role in democratizing access to the arts. By bringing performances into everyday spaces, dance becomes a visible and integral part of community life. This accessibility can demystify the art form, making it more relatable and less intimidating for those who might not have previous exposure to dance. Public performances can act as a catalyst for further engagement, inspiring viewers to seek out classes, workshops, and other dance-related activities. They also offer a platform for local dancers and choreographers to showcase their work, gaining recognition and support from their community.

Community Building through Dance

Dance has a powerful ability to bring people together, transcending boundaries of age, culture, and background. One of the most compelling ways this happens is through dance projects that involve diverse participants. These projects often see children, teenagers, adults, and seniors dancing side by side. This intergenerational mix not only enriches the experience for everyone involved but also fosters a deeper understanding between different age groups. For instance, young dancers may learn traditional dances from older participants, while seniors can stay active and engaged by learning contemporary styles from the younger generation.

Cultural exchange is another significant aspect of these inclusive dance projects. When individuals from various backgrounds come together to dance, they share their unique cultural expressions and traditions. This intercultural interaction promotes mutual respect and appreciation, breaking down stereotypes and prejudices. A community dance project might feature a blend of Latin, African, Asian, and Western dance forms, creating a vibrant tapestry that reflects the diversity of the participants. This cross-cultural exchange not only enhances the richness of the event but also strengthens social cohesion within the community.

Local dance events play a crucial role in stimulating community interest and pride. When a neighborhood hosts a dance festival or performance, it often attracts residents who might not typically take an interest in the arts. The excitement generated by such events can be infectious, drawing in audiences and participants alike. Through these events, communities can showcase their talents and cultural heritage, fostering a sense of pride among residents. Moreover, local businesses often benefit as well, with increased foot traffic and economic activity. Restaurants, cafes, and shops might see a boost in customers during these events, contributing to the overall economic growth of the area.

Dance education programs hosted by community centers are vital for enhancing the skill sets of residents and fostering a supportive environment for artistic development. These programs offer classes and workshops that cater to various skill levels, from beginners to advanced dancers. By providing accessible training opportunities, community centers help individuals develop their talents and explore their creativity. Additionally, these programs often emphasize the importance of discipline, teamwork, and perseverance, values that are transferable to other areas of life. A young dancer who learns the fundamentals of ballet or hip-hop at a community center might later apply those same principles of hard work and dedication to their academic or professional pursuits.

Participation in community dance activities fosters empathy and respect among attendees, facilitating harmonious interactions and reducing prejudices. When people come together to dance, they must rely on one another to succeed, whether it's coordinating steps, maintaining rhythm, or supporting each other during lifts and spins. This collaborative effort builds trust and camaraderie, encouraging participants to look beyond superficial differences and see each other as fellow human beings. As individuals work together towards a common goal, they develop a deeper sense of empathy and understanding, which can translate into more positive interactions in daily life.

Community dance events also have the potential to reduce social isolation, particularly among marginalized or underserved populations. For many, these gatherings provide a rare opportunity to connect with others and feel a sense of belonging. For instance, an elderly person living alone might find joy and companionship in a weekly dance class, while a newcomer to the community could make new friends through a neighborhood dance group. By offering an inclusive space where everyone is welcome, community dance initiatives can help bridge social divides and create a more cohesive society.

Bringing It All Together

Dance has the unique ability to bridge divides and build stronger, more united communities. By bringing people together through shared movement and expression, dance initiatives and workshops foster empathy, inclusivity, and mutual respect. These programs offer valuable opportunities for individuals of all backgrounds to connect, learn from one another, and celebrate their diverse cultures. Whether it is a mixed-ability workshop or an intergenerational project, participants gain a deeper appreciation for each other's contributions, creating a supportive and cohesive environment.

Moreover, public dance events and community programs play a vital role in enhancing the cultural and economic vitality of neighborhoods. Performances held in accessible spaces invite everyone to experience the joy and inspiration that dance brings, breaking down barriers and encouraging broader participation. By involving local residents and attracting visitors, these events can stimulate economic growth while promoting a sense of pride and connection within the community. Through continued support and engagement in dance initiatives, we can harness the power of dance to inspire positive change and create a more inclusive and harmonious world for all.

PART 5:

DANCE
Evolving &/+
Developing

Chapter 13:

Future Trends in Dance

Future trends in dance are reshaping the landscape of the industry, offering new opportunities and challenges for dancers, choreographers, and event promoters. With a continuous influx of innovative styles and technological advancements, the dance world is becoming a melting pot of creativity where traditional techniques merge with contemporary innovations. This dynamic evolution promises not only to redefine artistic expression but also to broaden the horizons for those passionate about making a mark in this vibrant field.

In this chapter, we will delve into various emerging dance styles, examining how the fusion of classical and modern forms is creating unique performances that captivate audiences. We'll also explore the significant role technology plays in transforming choreography and performance, from virtual reality experiences to motion capture precision. Furthermore, the impact of cultural exchange and interdisciplinary collaboration on dance will be highlighted, showcasing how these elements foster innovation and inclusiveness. By understanding these future trends, readers will gain valuable insights into preparing themselves for the evolving dance industry, ensuring they remain competitive and inspired in their artistic pursuits.

Emerging Dance Styles
The dance industry is evolving rapidly,

with new styles constantly emerging and shaping the future. One of the most exciting trends is the fusion of traditional and modern dance forms. This blend creates innovative performances that captivate audiences by combining the rich heritage of classical dance with the dynamism of contemporary movements.

Traditional dances have deep cultural roots and tell stories passed down through generations. Modern dance, on the other hand, emphasizes self-expression and often breaks away from established norms. When these two styles merge, dancers can create something truly unique. For example, a ballet dancer might incorporate hip-hop elements into their routine, leading to a performance that honors both the grace of ballet and the energy of hip-hop. This fusion not only broadens the dancer's skill set but also opens up new artistic possibilities.

To adapt to this trend, dancers should immerse themselves in various dance forms. Attending workshops, watching diverse performances, and practicing different styles will help them understand how to blend traditional techniques with modern innovations. Moreover, collaborating with dancers from other traditions can provide fresh perspectives and inspire creativity.

Another significant trend influencing dance today is technology. Advancements in technology are reshaping the way choreographers create and dancers perform. For instance, projection mapping can transform a simple stage into a dynamic environment, enhancing the storytelling aspect of a dance. Motion sensors can capture a dancer's movements and translate them into digital art, making the performance interactive and visually stunning.

Technology also plays a crucial role in reaching broader audiences. Social media platforms allow dancers to showcase their work globally, building a fanbase beyond geographical boundaries. Online dance classes make learning accessible to anyone with an internet connection, democratizing dance education. To stay ahead, dancers should familiarize themselves with these technologies and explore how they can be integrated into their practices.

One can't talk about future trends in dance without mentioning cultural exchange. In our increasingly globalized world, dancers have access to a plethora of cultural influences. Embracing these diverse styles can lead to the creation of unique and inclusive performances. For instance, a dancer might combine Indian Bharatanatyam with Brazilian Samba rhythms, resulting in an eclectic performance that celebrates both cultures.

Cultural exchange fosters a deeper appreciation for different traditions and can break down cultural barriers. Dancers who are open to learning from other traditions will find themselves more versatile and enriched. Participating in international festivals, collaborations, and residencies can provide invaluable opportunities to experience and integrate different cultural dance forms.

Interdisciplinary collaboration is another driving force behind the evolution of dance. Collaborations between dancers and artists from other disciplines such as music, visual arts, theater, and even science lead to the development of groundbreaking dance styles. For example, working with a musician can help a choreographer better understand rhythm and musicality, leading to more cohesive performances. Similarly, partnering with visual artists can result in innovative costume designs or stage setups that enhance the overall aesthetic of a performance.

To thrive in this collaborative environment, dancers should step out of their comfort zones and seek partnerships with artists from other fields. Networking events, interdisciplinary workshops, and joint projects are excellent ways to meet potential collaborators. By broadening their horizons, dancers can gain new insights and push the boundaries of what dance can achieve.

The Industry's Technological Evolution

Technological advancements are profoundly reshaping the dance industry, opening doors to new possibilities and experiences. One of the most exciting developments is the integration of Virtual Reality (VR) and Augmented Reality (AR). These technologies are creating immersive dance experiences that were once only imaginable in science fiction. By using VR headsets, audiences can now be transported to virtual stages where they can interact with dancers in completely new ways. AR, on the other hand, overlays digital elements onto the real world, allowing for interactive performances where virtual dancers can appear in physical spaces alongside live performers.

For instance, a choreographer could design a piece that involves both human dancers and holographic figures projected through AR technology. This combination creates an entirely new visual experience and offers endless creative possibilities. Imagine attending a dance show where the stage transforms dynamically, with stunning visuals synchronizing perfectly with the dancers' movements. Such innovations not only amplify the artistic expression of dance but also make it more accessible to wider audiences by breaking geographical barriers.

Motion capture technology is another game-changer in the realm of dance. Originally developed for animated movies and video games, this technology captures the intricate movements of dancers and translates them into digital characters. This allows for unprecedented precision in choreography and performance accuracy. Wearable sensors track every movement, enabling choreographers to analyze and perfect sequences down to the finest detail. It also makes it possible to create digital avatars that can perform complex routines exactly as intended, preserving the integrity of the choreography.

Moreover, motion capture technology opens up opportunities for creating dance routines that blend reality with fantasy. For example, a dancer's movements can be captured and then used to animate a fantastical creature or character in a virtual environment. This not only enhances the storytelling aspect of performances but also attracts a broader audience who may be interested in the technological aspects of the production.

Dance Teaching Business

The accessibility of dance education has been significantly enhanced by digital platforms. Online dance classes and tutorials have democratized access to high-quality instruction, making it possible for aspiring dancers from all over the world to learn from top professionals without having to relocate or spend large sums of money. Platforms like YouTube, Instagram, and specialized dance education websites offer a plethora of resources for dancers of all skill levels. Whether it's learning a new technique, practicing routines, or getting feedback from instructors, these digital tools have made dance education more flexible and inclusive.

Furthermore, digital platforms facilitate continuous learning and self-improvement. Dancers can easily revisit lessons, practice at their own pace, and connect with instructors and peers through virtual communities. This flexibility is particularly beneficial for those who may have other commitments, such as school or work, allowing them to pursue their passion for dance without compromising their other responsibilities.

Social media has also had a profound impact on the dance industry, changing the way dancers and choreographers share their work and connect with audiences. Platforms like TikTok and Instagram have become popular venues for showcasing dance routines and creative choreography. Hashtags and challenges enable dances to go viral, reaching millions of viewers in a matter of days. This exposure not only boosts the profiles of individual dancers but also promotes dance as an art form to a global audience.

Social media also fosters collaboration and innovation within the dance community. Dancers can easily share ideas, seek inspiration, and collaborate on projects despite being physically apart. Live streaming performances and virtual workshops have become commonplace, allowing dancers to interact with their audiences in real-time. This direct engagement helps build a loyal fan base and opens up new opportunities for monetization, such as sponsored content and online donations.

In addition, social media serves as a valuable tool for networking and career advancement. Dancers can connect with industry professionals, audition for roles, and find job opportunities through these platforms. It provides a space for dancers to market themselves, showcase their skills, and build a personal brand, which is crucial in today's competitive landscape.

By embracing these technological advancements, the dance industry is poised for a dynamic future. The possibilities are vast, from creating immersive performances with VR and AR to enhancing choreography with motion capture and making dance education more accessible through digital platforms. Social media continues to revolutionize how dance is shared and experienced, bringing the dance community closer together and expanding its reach.

As these technologies continue to evolve, they will undoubtedly lead to even more innovative and transformative practices in the dance world. Dancers, choreographers, educators, and event promoters must stay informed and adapt to these changes to thrive in this rapidly advancing field. Embracing technology not only enhances the artistic and educational aspects of dance but also ensures its continued growth and relevance in the modern era.

Adapting to Change through Innovation

In today's fast-evolving dance industry, dancers and choreographers need to equip themselves with a diverse set of skills and strategies to thrive. One key strategy is embracing cross-disciplinary skills. Gone are the days when mastering dance techniques alone was sufficient. Dancers now must delve into multimedia production, understanding how to create engaging video content that can be shared and marketed online. Skills in video editing, sound design, and even basic graphic design can significantly enhance a dancer's ability to stand out in a crowded digital landscape. Marketing skills are equally crucial— knowing how to build a personal brand, use social media effectively, and engage with audiences can turn passion into a sustainable career.

Sustainable practices in dance are becoming increasingly important as the industry moves towards more environmentally conscious choices. Whether you're a dancer or a choreographer, considering the environmental impact of costuming and stage design is essential. Opting for materials that are eco-friendly, such as sustainably-sourced fabrics or recycled materials, can make a huge difference. Additionally, reusing costumes and props, and choosing energy-efficient lighting for performances, helps in reducing the carbon footprint. These sustainable choices not only benefit the environment but also set a positive example for others in the industry to follow.

Lifelong learning is another cornerstone for thriving in the ever-changing world of dance. The importance of continuous education cannot be overstated. Staying updated with the latest dance trends, techniques, and emerging styles ensures that dancers remain relevant and competitive. This might involve taking workshops, attending masterclasses, or enrolling in specialized training programs. For choreographers, this could mean exploring new choreographic methods or integrating technology into their work. Lifelong learning keeps the mind agile and open to new possibilities, making it easier to adapt and innovate.

Networking and collaboration also play a pivotal role in fostering innovation and career growth within the dance community. Building strong connections with fellow dancers, choreographers, and industry professionals opens up numerous opportunities for collaborations and partnerships. These relationships can lead to joint projects, mentorship opportunities, and access to valuable resources. Engaging in collaborative work often results in fresh ideas and creative breakthroughs that might not emerge when working in isolation. Participating in dance festivals, competitions, and industry events is an excellent way to expand one's network and gain visibility.

Moreover, it's worth noting that the ability to collaborate extends beyond just connections within the dance industry. Interdisciplinary collaborations with artists from different fields—such as musicians, filmmakers, and visual artists—can lead to innovative performance pieces and unique artistic expressions. Such collaborations enrich the creative process and allow for the fusion of different art forms, resulting in more dynamic and engaging performances.

Final Thoughts

As we look toward the future of the dance industry, it's clear that adaptability and embracing innovation are key. The amalgamation of traditional and modern dance styles offers a rich palette for creativity, allowing dancers to forge new paths and create performances that intrigue and inspire. By immersing themselves in various dance forms, learning new techniques, and seeking interdisciplinary collaborations, dancers can expand their horizons and stay ahead in this ever-evolving landscape. Additionally, integrating technology into dance not only enhances artistic expression but also opens up opportunities to reach broader audiences and create immersive, engaging experiences.

Moreover, fostering cultural exchange and sustainable practices within the dance community paves the way for a more inclusive and environmentally conscious industry. Lifelong learning ensures that dancers and choreographers remain at the forefront of emerging trends and techniques, while networking and collaboration drive innovation and career growth. As dancers, instructors, and event promoters navigate this dynamic field, staying informed and adaptable will be essential to their success. By uniting passion with entrepreneurial skills, they can contribute to a vibrant, forward-thinking dance industry that continues to captivate and inspire.

Chapter 14:

Overcoming Challenges in the Dance Industry

Facing challenges in the dance industry is an integral part of every dancer's journey. From the painstaking hours spent perfecting a routine to the nerve-wracking moments before stepping onto a stage, each dancer encounters obstacles that test their resolve and passion. Life in dance demands perseverance, creativity, and the willingness to embrace growth through trials. While these challenges can seem overwhelming at times, they also hold the potential to unlock new levels of skill and self-awareness. As dancers push their limits and learn from setbacks, they not only refine their technical abilities but also cultivate resilience—a quality essential for thriving in this competitive field. By approaching hurdles with an optimistic mindset, dancers can transform what seems like adversity into opportunities for artistic evolution and personal development.

The path to overcoming challenges in the dance industry encompasses various aspects, including dealing with rejection and competition, maintaining physical and mental health, and balancing personal life with professional aspirations. In this chapter, we will explore how dancers navigate the tough reality of auditions and competitions, turning them into valuable learning experiences rather than deterrents. We'll delve into strategies for sustaining both body and mind amidst demanding practice schedules, highlighting the significance of rest, professional support, and mindfulness. The narrative will also address the art of balancing a dance career with personal life, stressing the importance of setting boundaries and building a supportive network. Each section aims to empower readers by offering insights and practical advice to not only survive but flourish in the world of dance. Through these discussions, you'll discover ways to confront and conquer the inevitable challenges of the industry, ultimately finding joy and fulfillment in your dance endeavors.

Dealing with Rejection and Competition

In the exhilarating world of dance, where each pirouette and leap is meticulously planned, dealing with rejection and competition can be daunting. However, it's crucial to understand that these experiences are not roadblocks but stepping stones in a dancer's journey. The inevitable "no" or criticism can be a powerful teacher if approached with an open mind. Every rejection offers an opportunity for introspection and growth. For instance, imagine attending a prestigious audition only to find your name missing from the callback list. Instead of dwelling on disappointment, use this moment to gather feedback. Maybe a mentor or fellow dancer noted areas needing improvement or perhaps there were elements of your audition that could have been enhanced. Embracing such feedback constructively helps to build resilience and refine skills, preparing you better for future opportunities.

It's easy to feel discouraged when abilities seem overshadowed by others', but it's important to remember that every dancer walks a unique path. To thrive amidst fierce competition, shifting perspective from comparison to personal development will help cultivate fulfillment in your dance career. Begin by setting individual goals that reflect your passion and strengths rather than measuring against the achievements of peers. This strategic approach encourages focusing energy on mastering new techniques, exploring distinct styles, or even experimenting with choreography. When progress is marked by personal milestones, each step forward becomes a celebration of individuality, enhancing both skill and confidence.

Moreover, nurturing a supportive community can significantly impact your journey in dance. Surrounding yourself with like-minded individuals who share similar aspirations creates a network of encouragement and constructive collaboration. Joining local dance groups, participating in workshops, or engaging in online forums allows dancers to connect with others who genuinely understand the struggles and triumphs of the industry. These connections provide more than just companionship; they offer a valuable exchange of ideas and feedback that propel everyone involved toward their goals. Take for example a group rehearsal setting where dancers openly discuss their experiences, providing each other with insights and fostering an environment ripe for creative innovation.

Additionally, having this support system means you have people to lean on during tougher times, such as auditions or competitions. It's about building relationships where positivity and motivation flow freely, turning challenges into experiences that strengthen bonds and improve emotional well-being. In cases where negativity arises, whether through harsh critiques or unconstructive comparisons, a strong community acts as a buffer, reminding each member of their worth and potential.

With determination and openness to learning, dancers can transform the daunting aspects of rejection and competition into meaningful lessons. Building resilience involves understanding that setbacks are temporary and often necessary for long-term success. Viewing rejection not as a personal failure but as an indication of where attention is most needed fosters an attitude geared toward continuous improvement. Similarly, keeping personal growth at the forefront of one's career relieves the pressure of outshining others, allowing room for genuine enjoyment and creativity in dance endeavors.

In turn, these mindsets contribute to sustainable career satisfaction, where dancers find joy and purpose in their art irrespective of external validation or accolades. Celebrating small victories, whether conquering a challenging routine or discovering new expressive ways through movement, feeds into an overall positive mindset. The journey itself becomes rewarding, as dancers remain driven by curiosity and the desire to evolve.

Maintaining Physical and Mental Health

In the vibrant world of dance, where every move is a blend of passion and precision, it can be easy to overlook the fundamental elements that keep dancers thriving: physical and mental well-being. Aspiring dancers often face the challenge of maintaining their artistry while balancing their health, which is crucial for a sustained career in the industry.

A pivotal aspect of this balance is managing training schedules wisely. The allure of perfecting routines and achieving peak performance can drive dancers to rigorous practice regimens. While dedication is admirable, it's important to recognize the body's need for rest. Overtraining is a common pitfall, leading to burnout, fatigue, and even injury. To prevent this, dancers should consider interspersing periods of intense training with adequate rest days. This not only aids in physical recovery but also enhances overall performance. Rest rejuvenates muscles, allowing them to repair and strengthen, thus preparing the body for future demands.

Take, for instance, the story of a young dancer who faced persistent injuries due to lack of rest. By integrating structured rest into her weekly schedule, she not only healed faster but also noticed improvements in her technique and endurance. This shift not only benefited her physically but also mentally, as she felt more motivated and less anxious about upcoming performances.

Another key component in sustaining a dancer's well-being is seeking professional support. Dancers are athletes, and like any athlete, they benefit from regular consultations with healthcare professionals. This includes physiotherapists who can provide tailored exercises to enhance strength and flexibility, and psychologists or counselors who can offer strategies for managing stress and anxiety. Understanding how to prevent injuries through proper technique and care can extend a dancer's career significantly. Moreover, addressing mental health needs ensures that dancers have the emotional resilience required to navigate the pressures of the industry.

While professional advice is invaluable, dancers can also incorporate mindfulness techniques into their daily routine as a personal tool for managing stress. Practices such as meditation and deep-breathing exercises are effective in calming the mind and centering focus. Mindfulness helps dancers stay grounded, particularly during high-pressure situations such as auditions or live performances. These practices encourage self-awareness and help in regulating emotions, thereby reducing performance anxiety.

Consider implementing a short meditation session each morning before starting the day's activities. Even five minutes can make a significant difference, helping to clear the mind and set a positive tone. Engaging in mindfulness can lead to enhanced concentration, enabling dancers to connect more deeply with their art and express their creativity fully.

Balancing the intensity of the dance world with moments of stillness and reflection creates the harmony necessary for a long and fulfilling career. Embracing mindfulness allows dancers to appreciate the journey rather than just the destination, fostering a healthy relationship with their craft.

To encapsulate, prioritizing both physical and mental well-being involves a multifaceted approach. Incorporating sufficient rest into training schedules is essential for avoiding burnout and injury. Regular check-ins with healthcare professionals equip dancers with the knowledge and tools to maintain their health proactively. Meanwhile, mindfulness practices such as meditation offer a sanctuary for mental clarity and emotional stability.

Balancing Personal Life and Career

Navigating the dance industry with its vibrancy and fast pace can be exhilarating yet overwhelming, particularly when balancing professional aspirations with personal life. Aspiring dancers often face challenges in maintaining this balance, but establishing clear boundaries is a key strategy that can guide them through.

Defining and maintaining boundaries between your professional and personal life is crucial amidst the hustle and bustle of a dance career. Imagine your work commitments as a stage light—you need it to perform, but it's important to know when to dim it to avoid being blinded by its intensity. Set specific times for rehearsals, performances, and other professional obligations, ensuring they do not encroach on your personal time. Use tools like calendars or scheduling apps to keep track of these commitments, and communicate your schedule clearly to both colleagues and loved ones. This helps prevent misunderstandings and fosters respect for your time from others. Regularly assessing your boundaries can also ensure they remain relevant and effective as your career progresses. Remember, boundaries are not limitations, but rather frameworks that support your personal well-being and long-term success.

In tandem with boundaries, prioritizing self-care activities outside of work is essential for combating fatigue and maintaining enthusiasm. Dancing requires a lot of physical energy, but mental fatigue can also creep in silently. Self-care goes beyond merely resting; it's an intentional practice of engaging in activities that rejuvenate your mind and body. This could mean setting aside time for hobbies unrelated to dance, such as reading, painting, or yoga. Physical rest is equally important—ensure you're getting adequate sleep, and consider integrating practices like meditation or gentle stretching routines to rejuvenate your body. These activities can help you recharge and approach each new day with renewed vigor. Finding joy in small moments outside of your dance world builds resilience, allowing you to tackle professional challenges with a fresh perspective.

Alongside self-care, open communication channels with loved ones form the backbone of a robust support network. The dance world can be isolating at times, with its competitive nature and demanding schedules. However, establishing a strong support system is indispensable. Share your experiences openly with family and friends, letting them in on your journey's ups and downs. This not only helps lighten emotional burdens but also strengthens relationships by fostering trust and understanding. Don't hesitate to lean on loved ones during tough times—whether it's sharing a quick chat over coffee, seeking advice, or even just enjoying mutual silence. Acknowledge their efforts in supporting you, and reciprocate when they require similar support. This reciprocal relationship nurtures a sense of belonging that buffers against the pressures of a demanding career.

Moreover, cultivating a supportive community within the dance industry itself can be an invaluable resource. Engage with fellow dancers, instructors, and industry professionals who share or understand the particular challenges you face. Attend workshops, networking events, and community gatherings to connect with individuals who can offer encouragement, mentorship, or collaboration opportunities. Such interactions not only expand your professional network but also provide a platform for sharing experiences and learning from others' journeys, further enriching your own path.

As you intertwine these strategies into your routine, remember that balance is dynamic and evolves with the different seasons of your life and career. What works today might need adjusting tomorrow. Stay open to re-evaluating your boundaries, self-care practices, and support systems as you grow both personally and professionally. Reflect on your progress regularly, celebrating your achievements and addressing areas needing adjustment with kindness and patience.

Final Thoughts

As we wrap up this chapter, it's important to reflect on the journey of overcoming challenges and setbacks in dance. We've explored how embracing rejection can lead to growth, with each critique offering a chance for self-improvement. By focusing on personal development rather than comparison, dancers can forge their unique paths, celebrating individuality instead of competing against others. Building a supportive community has also been highlighted as a key element, ensuring that dancers have a network to lean on during auditions or competitions. This sense of belonging not only provides emotional resilience but also fosters an environment where creativity and motivation thrive.

This chapter serves as a reminder that the dance world, while challenging, is also full of opportunities for those who navigate it with courage and openness. Setbacks should be seen as temporary obstacles, paving the way for long-term success when tackled with determination and a willingness to learn. By maintaining focus on personal growth and nurturing connections within the dance community, dancers can transform challenges into stepping stones toward a fulfilling career. Celebrating each achievement, no matter how small, enhances joy and purpose in the art of dance, ensuring that the journey itself remains rewarding and inspiring.

Chapter 15:

Continuing Education and Professional Development

Lifelong learning and growth are vital to thriving in the dance industry. This dynamic field, brimming with passion and creativity, requires a commitment to continuous education and professional development. For young adults eager to transform their love for dance into a viable career, staying current with new techniques and industry trends is essential. Aspiring dancers often find themselves at a crossroads where enthusiasm meets opportunity, highlighting the need for continued learning to stand out in a competitive environment. The ever-evolving nature of dance not only challenges performers to refine their skills but also invites them to embrace new styles and approaches. This pursuit transforms the act of dancing into a lifelong journey of exploration and mastery, driving both personal and professional advancement.

In this chapter, you will explore various avenues available for furthering your education in dance beyond the basics. From master classes and formal certifications to residencies and intensive programs, you'll discover how each path offers unique opportunities for enhancing your craft. These educational experiences provide more than just skills; they foster connections within the dance community, allow interaction with renowned professionals, and open doors to diverse career possibilities. You will also learn about the importance of balancing technical prowess with an understanding of dance theory and history, ensuring a well-rounded approach to your practice. Navigating through these opportunities equips you with the tools needed to adapt and innovate, setting you on a trajectory toward a fulfilling career in dance. Through a narrative lens, this chapter will guide you in recognizing how strategic educational choices can propel you toward success and resilience in the vibrant world of dance.

Opportunities for Advanced Training

In the dynamic world of dance, continuous learning and skill enhancement are not just options—they are necessary for growth and success. One powerful way to enrich your dance journey is by enrolling in master classes. These specialized sessions offer unique access to renowned professionals in the industry, giving dancers the chance to delve deeply into specific styles and techniques. Imagine standing in a room with a celebrated choreographer or a dancer from a famous troupe; their insights and expertise provide an invaluable opportunity to elevate your craft. For instance, a master class focused on contemporary ballet might introduce you to movements and stylistic nuances that aren't typically covered in regular classes, pushing your boundaries and expanding your artistic vocabulary.

Dance Teaching Business

Guidelines are essential when considering master classes. First, research the instructors' backgrounds and teaching styles to ensure alignment with your goals. Look for reviews from past participants to gain insight into what you can expect. Additionally, prepare questions in advance about techniques or concepts you're eager to learn more about. This proactive approach maximizes your learning experience, transforming each session into a stepping stone toward mastery.

While master classes are great for enhancing specific skills, pursuing formal certifications and degrees in dance represents a structured path to deepening your overall knowledge base. Beyond perfecting technique, these educational programs broaden your understanding of dance history, theory, and pedagogy. A certificate in dance education, for example, could open doors to teaching opportunities, allowing you to share your passion while further establishing your credibility within the field. Moreover, a degree might offer specializations in different genres— from jazz to hip-hop—making you a versatile performer capable of adapting to various styles and professional demands.

For aspiring dancers, especially those looking to merge entrepreneurial ambitions with their artistic pursuits, obtaining these qualifications can be a strategic move. By earning credentials, you're not only boosting your resume but also equipping yourself with a broader set of skills. This versatility is paramount in today's competitive dance market, where being able to jump seamlessly between styles often distinguishes successful professionals from the rest. When selecting a program, consider factors such as curriculum content, faculty expertise, and practical components like performance showcases or internships that align with your career aspirations.

Beyond classroom settings, participating in residencies and intensives offers immersive training experiences that can profoundly impact your development as a dancer. These programs often feature extended periods of concentrated study, providing a space to refine your performance skills through close guidance and creative collaboration. Imagine spending several weeks in a residency, surrounded by fellow dancers, choreographers, and artists dedicated to exploring innovative approaches. This environment not only hones technical abilities but also fosters a sense of community among participants, sparking new ideas and potential collaborations.

Residencies and intensives serve as laboratories for creativity, where experimentation is encouraged, and traditional boundaries are challenged. Engaging with diverse perspectives from both instructors and peers during these programs can lead to breakthroughs in your understanding of movement, musical interpretation, and personal artistry. To make the most of these experiences, enter them with an open mind and a willingness to step outside your comfort zone. Set personal objectives before commencing—whether mastering a particular sequence or developing a new choreographic piece—and actively seek feedback to guide your progress.

The benefits of these avenues for continuous improvement are manifold. Each initiative—be it attending a master class, pursuing formal education, or diving into a residency—contributes uniquely to your growth as a dancer. Master classes sharpen specific techniques, certifications lend academic weight and versatility, while residencies immerse you in environments ripe for creative exploration.

Together, they form a comprehensive strategy for lifelong learning within the dance industry.

Staying Updated with Industry Trends

In the fast-paced and always changing world of dance, staying current with industry trends is key to success. Being informed about new styles, techniques, and audience preferences can give aspiring dancers and professionals alike a competitive edge. One effective way to stay ahead in this dynamic landscape is by following industry publications. These resources are rich with insights into upcoming styles and influences, often predicting shifts in market demands and audience preferences. By keeping up with these publications, you not only stay informed but also gain a better understanding of what might attract audiences and potential clients.

Moreover, industry publications offer a window into varied perspectives from seasoned professionals and thought leaders in dance. Articles and interviews often reveal how these experts navigate changes and adapt their craft, providing valuable lessons for those looking to thrive in the field. Engaging regularly with such content fosters a habit of continuous learning, encouraging readers to innovate and adapt their skills continuously.

Another vital method of staying updated is attending conferences and seminars. These gatherings provide an immersive experience where new technologies and techniques are showcased. Workshops and demonstrations often accompany these events, offering participants hands-on opportunities to engage with cutting-edge tools and methods. This direct exposure to innovations can significantly enhance one's technical abilities and broaden creative horizons.

Conferences and seminars also serve as platforms for learning from experts who share their insights and experiences in the industry. Participants can attend panel discussions, keynote speeches, and breakout sessions tailored to various aspects of dance and performance. The diversity of topics covered ensures that there's something for everyone, whether you're interested in choreography, production, or artistic direction. Moreover, these events facilitate collaboration on future projects, enabling like-minded individuals to connect and explore potential partnerships.

Networking is another significant benefit of attending these functions. Meeting peers from different geographical locations and backgrounds expands one's professional network and opens doors to unique opportunities. Collaborating with other artists and event promoters not only enriches your own work but also helps build a supportive community that values shared growth and development.

Engaging with online communities further enhances one's ability to stay relevant in the dance world. These digital spaces offer global networking opportunities, allowing dancers to interact with colleagues from around the world. Platforms like social media groups, forums, and specialized dance websites host countless discussions where members can share experiences, seek advice, and showcase their work. This exchange of information creates a vibrant environment where ideas flow freely, fostering creativity and innovation.

Being part of an online community also provides a platform for feedback and recognition. Dancers can post videos of their performances, choreographies, or practice sessions and receive constructive criticism from seasoned professionals and fellow enthusiasts. This feedback loop is crucial for growth, as it highlights areas of improvement while also acknowledging strengths.

Online communities often feature challenges, collaborations, and virtual performances, which can be instrumental in gaining visibility and experience. Participating in these activities not only hones one's skills but also builds confidence by performing in front of a wider audience. Additionally, the global reach of these platforms means that talents are recognized beyond local or national borders, creating pathways for international career opportunities.

For those turning their passion into a business venture, engaging with these communities provides insights into effective marketing strategies and brand building. Observing how others present themselves and their work offers inspiration and practical knowledge on crafting a personal brand that resonates with audiences and clients alike.

Attending Workshops and Conferences

In the dynamic dance industry, hands-on learning experiences and professional networking play pivotal roles in propelling dancers into successful careers. For young adults aspiring to carve a niche in this field, it's essential to engage actively with these growth opportunities. Not only do they provide practical knowledge and skill enhancement, but they also foster creativity and build crucial relationships within the community.

Let's start by delving into the world of choreography workshops. These immersive environments offer an invaluable chance for dancers to expand their creative horizons. By experimenting with various movement styles, participants learn to push beyond conventional boundaries, unlocking new potential in their performances. Choreography workshops often bring together seasoned instructors who provide personalized feedback. This guidance helps dancers refine their techniques and understand how best to convey emotion and narrative through their movements.

Imagine a dancer accustomed to contemporary forms taking their first plunge into the intricate patterns of hip-hop or the fluidity of modern ballet. Such exposure not only broadens their repertoire but also enhances their adaptability— a key asset in any performance scenario. Workshops encourage experimentation, allowing dancers to make bold interpretations and discover unique styles that could set them apart in auditions.

Moving on to the importance of networking at dance conferences, we find a realm ripe with opportunities for young professionals. Conferences serve as melting pots for talent, where connections form and grow organically. Meeting fellow artists, industry leaders, and potential collaborators can open doors previously unimaginable. These gatherings are not merely about exchanging business cards; they are about building relationships that matter.

By actively participating in discussions and presentations at conferences, dancers can showcase their talents beyond the confines of a stage. Whether it's through impromptu performances or engaging conversations, demonstrating one's passion and skills can capture the attention of influential figures who might offer future collaborations. Attendees leave these events not just with insights into industry trends but with a vibrant network ready to support and amplify their careers.

Now, consider the myriad possibilities presented by participation in dance festivals. Every festival is a stage, each one offering distinct experiences across diverse settings. For dancers, this is not just about performing; it's about immersion in a vibrant cultural exchange. Festivals tend to draw artists from all corners of the globe, facilitating collaboration with individuals whose backgrounds and styles vary widely. This enriches a dancer's perspective and hones their ability to work harmoniously within eclectic ensembles.

At these festivals, dancers gain exposure to different audiences and potential clients, further paving the way for career advancement. The platform allows for the showcasing of individual talent while also fostering valuable lessons in teamwork and adaptability—skills vital for any professional journey. Engaging in such events encourages participants to consider performance from alternate perspectives, enhancing their versatility.

These experiences collectively serve as catalysts for personal and professional development. They prepare dancers not just to perform but to innovate, adapt, and thrive amid the challenges of a competitive industry. Aspiring dancers who embrace hands-on learning and seize networking opportunities position themselves favorably in the ever-evolving dance landscape.

Moreover, engaging with these avenues cultivates a mindset of lifelong learning. The dance industry, much like any creative field, is subject to constant change and reinvention. Staying ahead requires readiness to learn continuously, absorbing new influences, and incorporating them into one's craft. Workshops, conferences, and festivals are not merely events— they are stepping stones towards a more informed, inspired, and interconnected career path.

For instructors and event promoters, these venues offer significant value too. Dance teachers expand their pedagogical approaches by participating in workshops and observing emerging trends. They return to their studios with fresh methods that inspire students and enhance classes. Event promoters benefit by witnessing firsthand what captivates audiences, helping them curate experiences that resonate deeply and attract larger crowds.

Incorporating these experiences into one's routine fuels both immediate and long-term success. Dancers find themselves equipped with robust portfolios brimming with innovation and diversity. They forge meaningful connections that blossom into fruitful partnerships, ensuring their profession does not remain static but blossoms dynamically.

For those seeking to transform their passion for dance into viable business ventures, understanding and harnessing these opportunities is crucial. By investing time and energy into workshops, conferences, and festivals, individuals foster environments conducive to creativity, collaboration, and growth. This approach not only benefits individual careers but elevates the entire community, driving the dance industry forward.

Insights and Implications

Throughout this chapter, we've explored the integral role of lifelong learning and growth within the dance industry. For young dancers and professionals eager to carve out a successful career, embracing continuous education is key. From master classes with industry luminaries to formal education that broadens your technical and theoretical understanding, every opportunity adds depth to your craft. Residencies and intensives further fuel this journey by fostering creativity and collaboration in immersive settings. Each experience encourages dancers to push their boundaries and unlock new potential, setting the stage for innovation and adaptability—qualities essential in the ever-evolving world of dance.

As we consider these opportunities, it's clear that staying informed about industry trends through publications, conferences, and online communities is equally vital. By keeping up-to-date with new styles and techniques, and connecting with like-minded individuals, dancers can thrive despite challenges. These avenues not only enhance skills but also offer insights into effective marketing strategies, helping dancers turn their passion into a fulfilling business venture. Ultimately, embracing these facets of growth cultivates a mindset poised for success—one ready to transform dreams into reality in the vibrant landscape of dance.

Chapter 16:

The Art, The Business, & The Academic Legacy.

The Artistic Mind/Heart & The Commercial Mentality + The Pedagogic Spirit

Points & Remarks for the **Entrepreneurial Artist**

The artist's mind and the business mind are often perceived as contrasting yet complementary forces that can drive creativity, innovation, and success. Understanding the nuances of each mindset can help individuals harness their unique strengths and collaborate effectively with others.

The Artist's Mind

1. **Creativity and Imagination**: At the heart of the artist's mind lies an intrinsic drive to create and imagine. Artists are often inspired by the world around them, expressing abstract concepts, emotions, and narratives through various mediums such as painting, music, writing, or performance.

2. **Intuition and Spontaneity**: Artists tend to rely heavily on intuition and often embrace spontaneity. They value the process of creation as much as the final product, allowing ideas to evolve organically without rigid structure.

3. **Emotion and Expression**: Emotional depth and expression are core to the artist's mindset. Artists often seek to evoke responses and provoke thought, using their work as a conduit for personal and collective exploration.

4. **Risk-Taking**: Creative endeavors inherently involve a level of risk. Artists are frequently

willing to push boundaries and challenge conventions, even at the cost of commercial viability.

5. **Subjectivity:** The artist's perspective is deeply personal and subjective. They view the world through a unique lens, often prioritizing individual interpretation and meaning over universal applicability.

The Business Mind

1. **Strategy and Planning**: A key characteristic of the business mind is its strategic approach. Business professionals analyze market trends, assess risks, and develop comprehensive plans to achieve long-term objectives.

2. **Analytical Thinking**: Rationality and logical analysis are paramount. The business mind uses data and evidence-based decision-making to drive growth, efficiency, and profitability.

3. **Efficiency and Productivity**: Businesses thrive on maximizing efficiency and productivity. Streamlined processes, cost management, and

performance metrics are crucial to achieving success in the business world.

4. **Risk Management**: While businesses also engage in risk-taking, it is often calculated and mitigated through strategic planning. The focus is on minimizing potential downsides while maximizing opportunities for growth.

5. **Objectivity**: The business perspective values objectivity and scalability. Decisions are made based on their potential to impact broader markets and achieve collective goals, often prioritizing empirical results over individual subjectivity.

Bridging the Gap

1. **Collaboration**: Successful ventures often require a synergy between the artist and business minds. Collaborating brings together the creative innovation of artists with the strategic acumen of business professionals, fostering comprehensive solutions and dynamic growth.

2. **Balanced Approach**: Embracing both mindsets can lead to a balanced approach where

creativity is nurtured within a structured, strategic framework. This balance can drive sustainable success, allowing for both artistic integrity and commercial viability.

3. **Innovation and Execution**: Innovation thrives at the intersection of art and business. Artistic creativity generates groundbreaking ideas, while business acumen ensures these ideas are effectively executed and brought to market.

In Resume

The artist's mind and the business mind embody distinct yet interdependent qualities. By appreciating and integrating these diverse perspectives, individuals and organizations can unlock new possibilities, drive innovation, and achieve holistic success. Understanding and valuing the contributions of both artistic and business mindsets allow for a richer, more comprehensive approach to creative and commercial endeavors.

Dancing for Both; for Passion & Compensation

Dancing for Business: The Unseen Synergy between Art and Enterprise

In an era characterized by rapidly shifting markets, emerging technologies, and the relentless pursuit of innovation, businesses are constantly seeking unique strategies to gain a competitive edge. One such unorthodox and often overlooked approach is the integration of dance into business operations and strategies. At first glance, dancing and business may seem worlds apart. One is rooted in artistic expression and physical movement, while the other is guided by metrics, profitability, and strategic planning. However, upon deeper examination, the incorporation of dance into a business setting reveals significant, multifaceted benefits. This essay explores how the art of dancing can enhance leadership, teamwork, creativity, and overall corporate culture.

Dance as a Metaphor for Leadership

Dance, specially forms like ballet, contemporary, and ballroom, demands a high degree of discipline, leadership, and the ability to both lead and follow—a direct parallel to effective business leadership. In ballroom dancing, for example, the leader sets the direction and guides their partner with subtle cues, akin to how a corporate leader steers their team towards achieving organizational goals. Leaders who engage in dance can better understand the nuances of body language, non-verbal communication, and the importance of clear, consistent guidance. This heightened awareness and skill in precise communication can translate directly into more effective leadership in the boardroom.

Enhancing Teamwork and Collaboration

Dancing is inherently collaborative; it requires trust, synchronization, and a mutual understanding of shared goals. These principles mirror those needed for successful business teams. Team-building exercises built around dance can break down hierarchical barriers, foster open communication, and build trust among employees. By participating in dance, team members learn to rely on one another, become more attuned to each other's strengths and weaknesses, and develop a rhythm for working together cohesively. This improved teamwork can lead to increased productivity and a more harmonious workplace.

Fostering Creativity and Innovation

The fluidity and freedom of expression inherent in dance unlock creative potential, which is essential for innovation in business. When employees engage in dance, they are encouraged to think outside of conventional confines, explore new ideas, and see problems from different perspectives. Dancing can serve as a powerful tool for brainstorming sessions, helping to loosen mental blocks and promote a culture of creative thought. Companies that nurture such creative environments are often better equipped to adapt to change and come up with breakthrough solutions.

Enhancing Corporate Culture and Employee Well-Being

Corporate culture sets the tone for every aspect of an organization's functioning, from employee morale to customer satisfaction. Incorporating dance into the workplace can significantly enhance this culture. Offering dance classes or organizing dance events can boost employee morale, reduce stress, and improve overall mental health. These activities provide employees with an enjoyable break from routine tasks, promoting a healthier work-life balance. Moreover, a culture that embraces such holistic activities reflects a company's commitment to employee well-being, further attracting and retaining top talent.

Real-world Applications

Several forward-thinking companies have already recognized the benefits of incorporating dance into their corporate framework. Google, for instance, offers dance sessions to its employees as part of its wellness program. These sessions not only provide health benefits but also serve as a creative outlet, sparking innovation. Similarly, organizations like Zappos focus on creating a fun and enjoyable workplace where activities like dance are part of everyday work culture, leading to high employee satisfaction and loyalty.

In Summary

The synergy between dancing and business is a testament to the growing recognition that soft skills, creativity, and human-centric approaches are invaluable in today's corporate landscape. By integrating dance into their operations, businesses can foster stronger leadership, enhance teamwork, spur innovation, and cultivate a vibrant corporate culture. As we move forward in an ever-evolving market, those who dare to blend the art of dance with business acumen may well find themselves dancing to the rhythm of success.

The Artist as a Teacher: Five Essential Principles for Success

Teaching, at its highest level, is an art form. Like painting, music, dance, or writing, it requires intuition, discipline, imagination, emotional intelligence, and deep human connection. When an artist becomes a teacher, education transforms from the delivery of information into a living, creative experience. The artist-teacher does not merely instruct; they inspire, awaken curiosity, and cultivate meaning.

In an era where education often emphasizes efficiency, testing, and outcomes, the perspective of the artist as a teacher offers something profoundly necessary: humanity. The artist-teacher approaches learning as a creative journey rather than a mechanical process. Success in this role depends on several foundational principles that unite artistic practice with effective pedagogy.

Here are 5 primary and important points that define success for the artist (Dancer) as a teacher:

1. Teaching as a Creative Practice

For the artist-teacher, teaching is not separate from art—it *is* art.

Just as artists respond to their materials, environment, and audience, effective teachers respond creatively to their students. Lessons are not rigid scripts but evolving compositions shaped by curiosity, dialogue, and experimentation. The classroom becomes a studio where ideas are sketched, revised, discarded, and rediscovered.

Creative teaching encourages flexibility. When students struggle, the artist-teacher adapts. When inspiration arises, it is welcomed. This openness models the artistic process itself—one that values exploration over perfection and growth over finality.

Success emerges when teaching is approached not as repetition, but as continuous creation.

2. Cultivating Curiosity Rather Than Control

Artists thrive on questions, not answers. Likewise, powerful teaching begins with curiosity.

The artist-teacher understands that learning deepens when students are invited to ask "why," "how," and "what if." Instead of positioning themselves as the sole authority, they function as guides—creating space for inquiry, discovery, and personal interpretation.

By reducing excessive control and embracing uncertainty, the teacher empowers students to become active participants rather than passive recipients. This approach nurtures intrinsic motivation and lifelong learning.

When curiosity becomes central, education shifts from obligation to exploration—a key marker of true success.

3. Emotional Intelligence and Human Connection

Art speaks to emotion, and teaching is fundamentally relational.

An artist-teacher recognizes that learning does not occur in isolation from feelings. Confidence, fear, joy, frustration, and self-doubt all shape the educational experience. Success therefore depends on emotional awareness, empathy, and trust.

By listening deeply and responding compassionately, the teacher creates a psychologically safe environment where students feel valued. Such safety allows risk-taking—an essential element in both art-making and learning.

Human connection transforms instruction into mentorship and classrooms into communities.

4. Modeling the Creative Life

Students learn as much from who a teacher *is* as from what they teach.

The artist-teacher models discipline, vulnerability, resilience, and passion. They demonstrate that creativity involves failure, revision, patience, and persistence. By sharing their own process—successes and struggles alike—they demystify excellence and make growth attainable.

This authenticity teaches students that creativity is not talent alone, but commitment to practice. Seeing a teacher actively engaged in creative thinking encourages students to trust their own voices and value their unique perspectives.

Success is magnified when teaching becomes a living example rather than a distant ideal.

5. Inspiring Purpose and Meaning

Beyond technique or content, the artist-teacher addresses the deeper question: *Why does this matter?*

Art has always been a vehicle for meaning, reflection, and social understanding. When teachers connect learning to identity, culture, ethics, and imagination, education gains relevance beyond the classroom.

The artist-teacher helps students see knowledge as a tool for expression, transformation, and contribution. This sense of purpose fuels perseverance and empowers learners to view themselves as creators within the world—not merely consumers of information.

True success is achieved when students leave not only informed, but inspired.

Topic Conclusion: Teaching as Living Art

The artist as a teacher embodies the union of creativity and responsibility. Through imagination, curiosity, empathy, authenticity, and purpose, education becomes more than instruction—it becomes transformation.

The five essential principles outlined in this chapter—

1. Teaching as creative practice
2. Cultivating curiosity
3. Emotional intelligence
4. Modeling the creative life
5. Inspiring meaning and purpose

form a foundation for lasting impact.

When teachers teach as artists, they do more than transfer knowledge. They shape thinkers, nurture vision, and awaken possibility. In doing so, they affirm that education, like art itself, is not merely about producing results—but about becoming fully human.

CONCLUSION

In the journey **through this book**, we've explored a vast and vibrant landscape filled with movement, rhythm, and endless opportunities. From the very first step onto the dance floor to the final bow at a sold-out event, each chapter has guided you through essential knowledge and skills necessary for a successful career in dance.

For young adults dreaming of a life where their passion drives their profession, these pages have illuminated the path. We've delved into the intricacies of the dance industry, shedding light on the many avenues one can explore. Whether it's performing on stage, teaching others, or organizing magnificent dance events, the dance world offers a multitude of ways to turn your passion into a thriving career.

Starting with understanding the dance industry's current state, you've learned about its many facets. The industry is dynamic and ever-evolving, influenced by cultural trends and technological advancements. Recognizing these factors allows you to adapt and stay ahead of the curve. You've seen how crucial it is to remain versatile and open-minded, always ready to embrace new styles and techniques.

Mastering performances is another crucial aspect we've covered. Beyond just the technical skills, you've discovered the importance of storytelling through dance. Conveying emotions and narratives with your body is what truly sets great dancers apart. You've experienced the significance of discipline, dedication, and continuous practice. Hard work pays off, and every moment spent honing your craft brings you closer to mastery.

For those aspiring to teach, becoming an effective dance instructor requires more than just knowing the steps. It's about understanding your students, inspiring them, and nurturing their growth. An excellent instructor ignites passion in their students, making learning enjoyable and rewarding. You've learned strategies to connect with various age groups and skill levels, ensuring that each student feels valued and motivated.

Organizing successful dance events has its own set of challenges and rewards. Through our exploration, you've gained insights into planning, promotion, and execution. From small community recitals to grand international competitions, the principles of event management remain consistent. Attention to detail, strong organizational skills, and a clear vision are key components. You've understood how to create experiences that leave lasting impressions on audiences and participants alike. Throughout this book, one underlying theme has been the power of community. Dance, at its core, is a shared experience. Building networks, collaborating with others, and fostering supportive environments are vital. Whether you're connecting with fellow dancers, engaging with students, or reaching out to potential clients and sponsors, relationships are the foundation of success. Your journey is enriched by the people you meet and the connections you make along the way.

Remember, the world of dance is as much about personal growth as it is about professional development. Every audition, every class, every performance teaches you something new. Embrace each opportunity with enthusiasm and a willingness to learn. Setbacks and failures are stepping stones to greatness. They build resilience and provide invaluable lessons that shape your future successes.

As you move forward, keep your goals in sight but remain flexible. The dance industry, like any creative field, is unpredictable. Trends shift, demands change, and opportunities arise in unexpected places. Adaptability will be your greatest ally. Stay curious, continue learning, and welcome innovation. Your unique combination of talent, hard work, and entrepreneurial spirit will set you apart.

To the young dancers reading this, your journey is just beginning. The passion that drives you is your most potent asset. Combine it with the knowledge and skills you've gained, and the world is yours to conquer. Be bold, be fearless, and let your love for dance guide you to extraordinary heights.

For the dance instructors, your role is pivotal. You are the mentors who shape the next generation of dancers. Your influence extends beyond the studio, instilling confidence, discipline, and creativity in your students. Your dedication to your craft and your students' success is commendable. Continue to inspire and lead with kindness and expertise.

Event promoters, your ability to bring people together through dance is a gift. Creating memorable events that celebrate dance not only entertains but also fosters a sense of community. Your efforts help to elevate the profile of dance and provide platforms for talent to shine. Keep pushing boundaries and introducing innovative ideas to make each event better than the last.

In conclusion, the dance world is brimming with opportunities for those willing to pursue their dreams with determination and passion. Whether you're on stage, in the studio, or behind the scenes, your contributions are invaluable. The knowledge and skills you've acquired from this book will serve as a solid foundation upon which to build your career.

As we close this chapter, remember that the end of this book is not the end of your journey. It is merely a stepping stone towards a future filled with potential. Keep dancing, keep learning, and keep striving for excellence. The world needs your talent, your creativity, and your passion. So, go out there and make your mark in the dance industry. Embrace the challenges, celebrate the victories, and never forget why you started this journey in the first place. Dance, after all, is not just a profession; it's a way of life.

About the Author

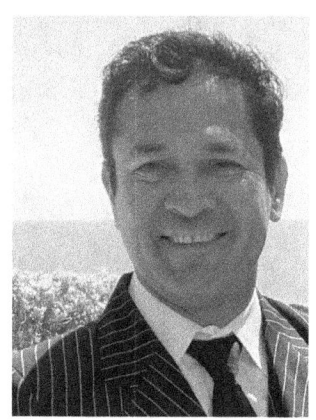

José E. Espinoza
Dance Instructor, Author, & Tango Event
Organizer
In the city of Los Angeles, CA

The Author commitment is to <u>Enjoy Life
Purpose</u>, Instructing, Guiding and Mentoring
others; to accomplish their Pasion or Vocation.
Jose's vison is to promote Art and
Entrepreneurships. Creating a Legacy through
his experience and expertise for the generation
to come

Other Books from The Author

Tango TAXIDANCER → Available on **Amazon**

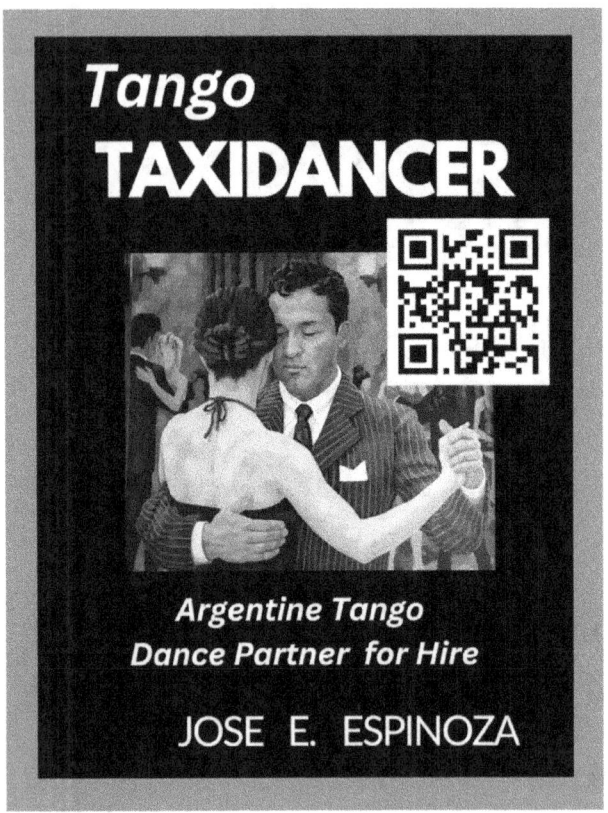

https://a.co/d/3kzDlHE

TANGO ABC 1.Com → Available on Amazon

Print Version Only → https://a.co/d/c47e7kI

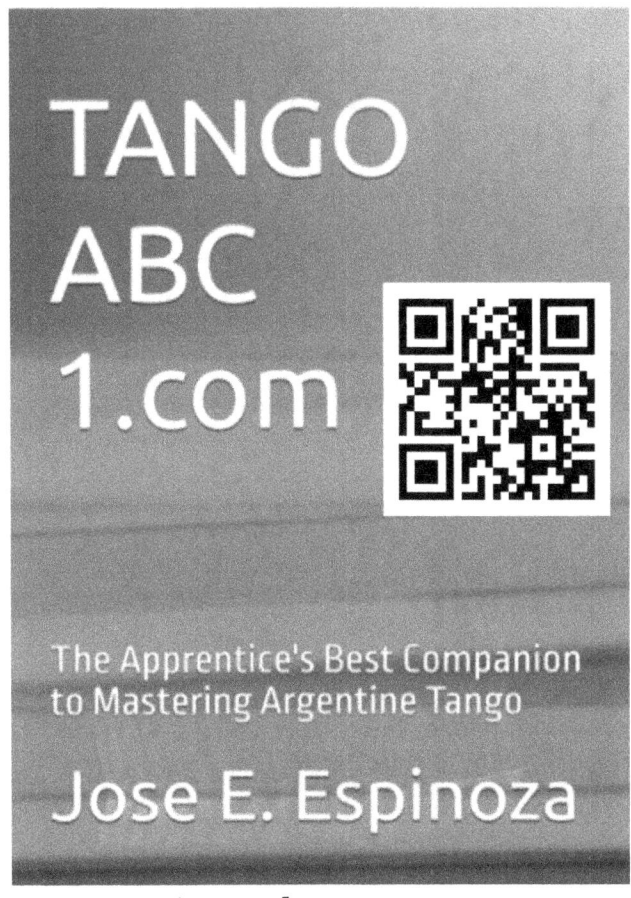

Print Version Only
https://a.co/d/c47e7kI

Dance Writer You.Inc → Available on Amazon

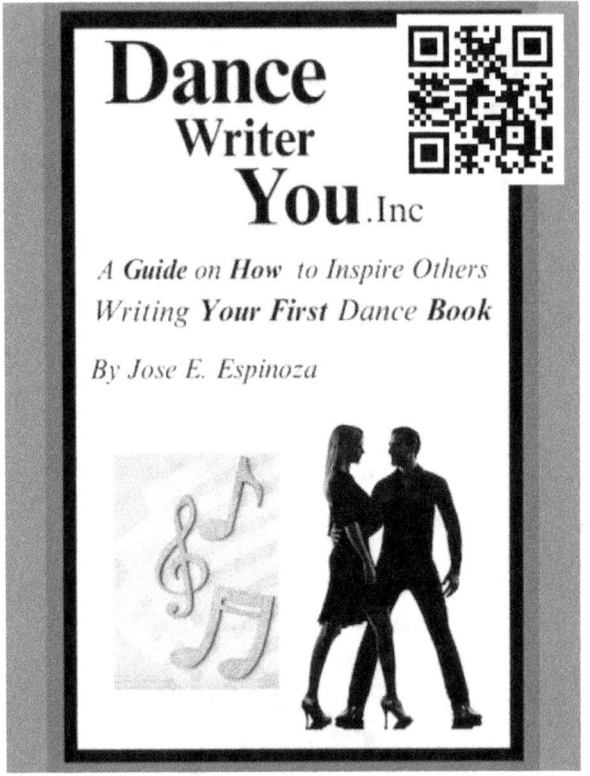

https://a.co/d/fMPSW1B

The End

Thank you for your Support

Your Recommendation/Referral of this Book to
Others
Will be greatly Appreciated

www.ingramcontent.com/pod-product-compliance
Lightning Source LLC
Chambersburg PA
CBHW071254220526
45468CB00001B/126